# Street Atlas of RICHMOND UPON THAMES KINGSTON

C000184698

## Key to Maps

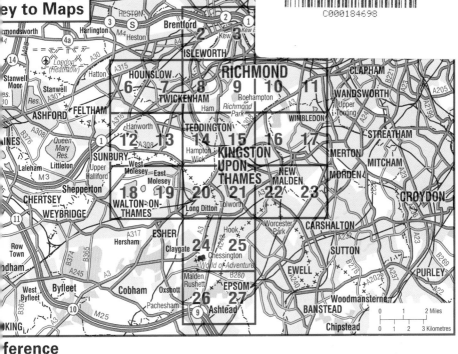

## Reference

| | | | | | | | |
|---|---|---|---|---|---|---|---|
| Motorway | M25 | Track | ====== | Church or Chapel | † |
| Road | A4 | Footpath | ------ | Fire Station | ■ |
| Under Construction | | Residential Walkway | ·········· | Hospital | ⊞ |
| Proposed | | Railway — Level Crossing / Station | ✕ | House Numbers — A & B Roads only | 246 / 213 |
| Road | B369 | Built Up Area | BROOK ST. | Information Centre | ⓘ |
| Dual Carriageway | | County Boundary | ·—·—· | National Grid Reference | ⁵20 |
| One Way A Roads — flow is indicated by a heavy line on the Drivers left. | → | District Boundary | ·—·—· | Police Station | ▲ |
| | | Posttown Boundary — By arrangement with the Post Office | | Post Office | ★ |
| Pedestrianized Road | ⌐======⌐ | Postcode Boundary — Within Posttown | | Toilet — With Facilities for the Disabled | ♿ |
| Restricted Access | | Map Continuation | 🔺 10 | | |

## Scale

**1:19,000**
**3.33 inches to 1 mile**

0 ¼ ½ ¾ Mile
0 250 500 750 Metres 1 Kilometre

### Geographers' A-Z Map Co. Ltd.

Head Office : Fairfield Road, Borough Green, Sevenoaks, Kent TN15 8PP  Telephone 01732 781000
Showrooms : 44 Gray's Inn Road, Holborn, London WC1X 8HX  Telephone 0171-242-9246

The Maps in this Atlas are based upon the Ordnance Survey 1 :10,560 Maps with the permission of the Controller of Her Majesty's Stationery Office
© Crown Copyright
© EDITION 1 1995   Copyright of the Publishers

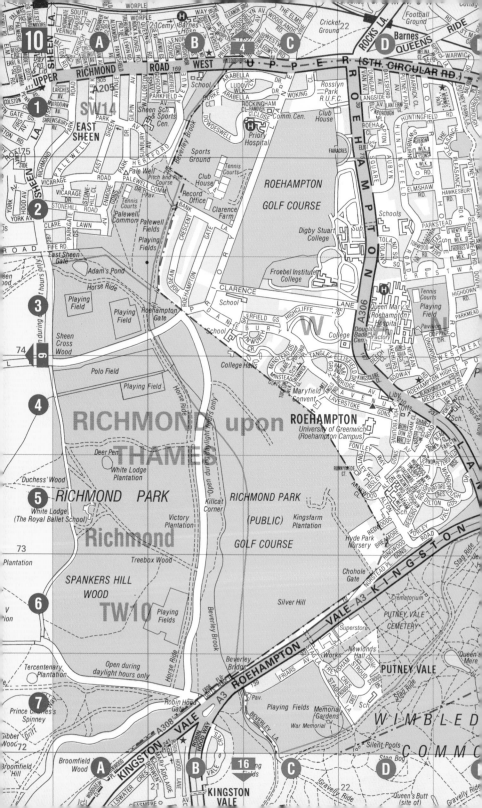

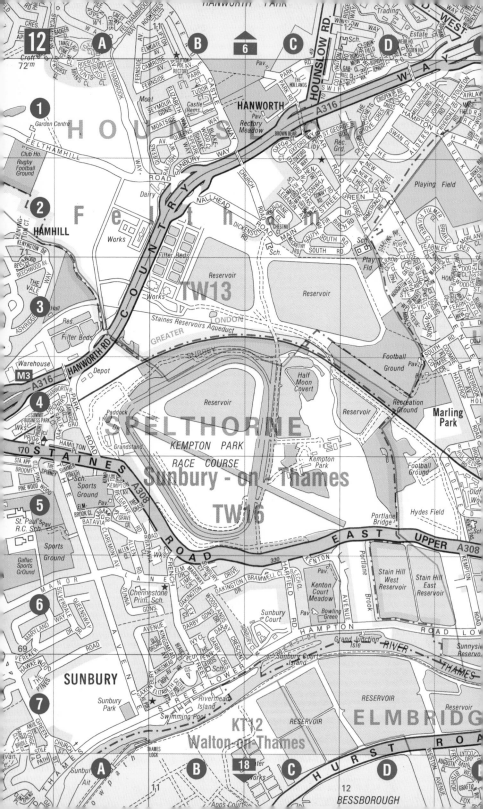

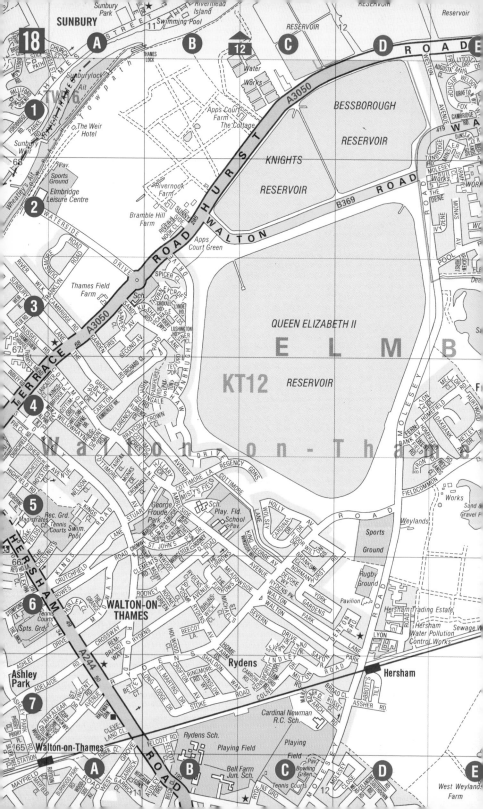

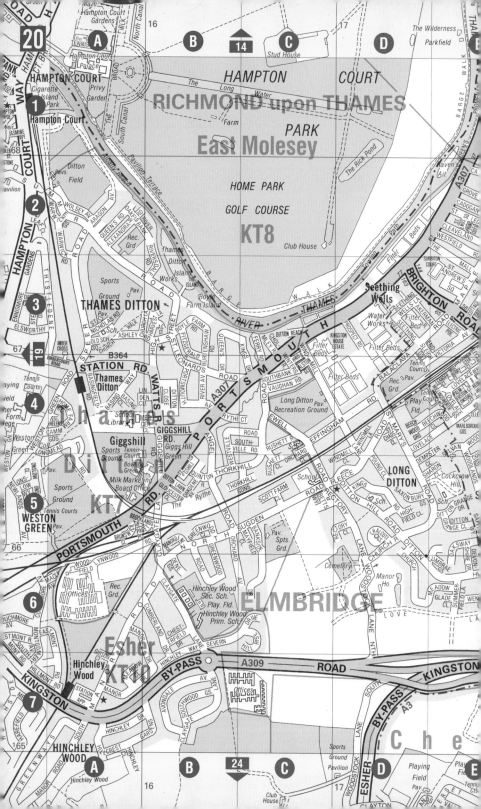

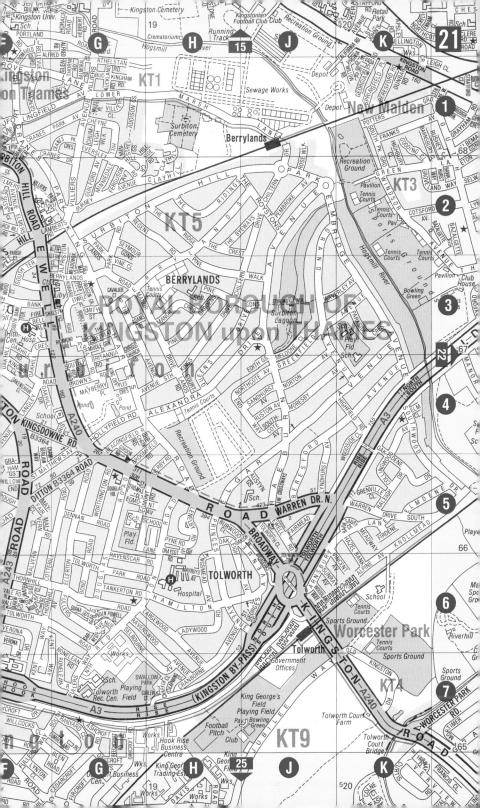

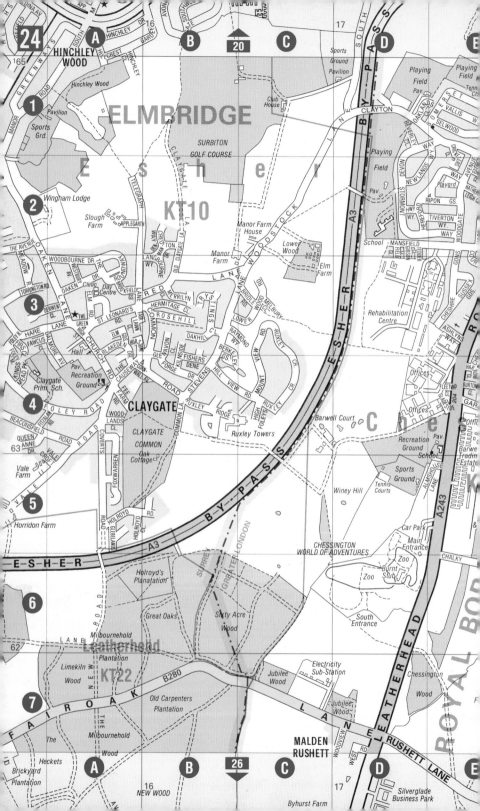

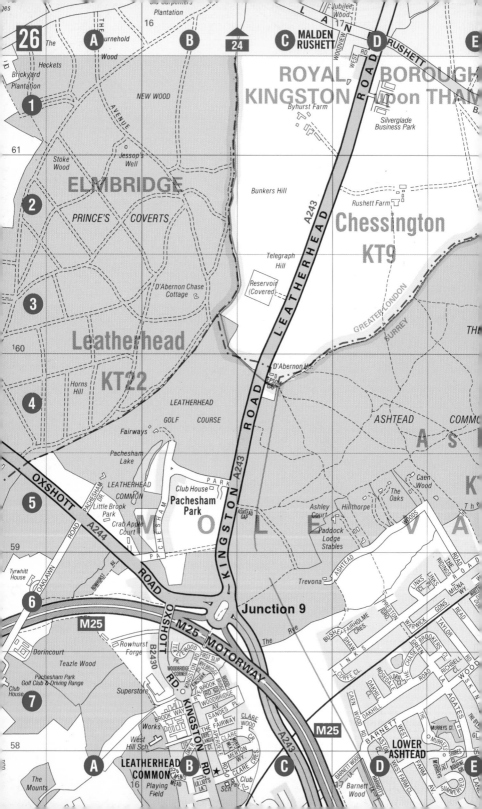

# INDEX TO STREETS

## HOW TO USE THIS INDEX

1. Each street name is followed by its Posttown or Postal Locality and then by its map reference; e.g. Abbotsbury Rd. Mord —2K **23** is in the Morden Pos and is to be found in square 2K on page **23**. The page number being shown in bold type.
A strict alphabetical order is followed in which Av., Rd., St., etc. (though abbreviated) are read in full and as part of the street name; e.g. Bank St. appea after Bankside Clo. but before Barfield.

2. Streets and a selection of Subsidiary names not shown on the Maps, appear in the index in *Italics* with the thoroughfare to which it is connected shown in brackets; e.g. *Adam Wlk. SW6 —4F 5 (off Crabtree La.)*

3. With the now general usage of Postcodes for addressing mail, it is not recommended that this index is used for such a purpose.

## GENERAL ABBREVIATIONS

| | | | | |
|---|---|---|---|---|
| All : Alley | Chyd : Churchyard | Gdns : Gardens | Mans : Mansions | Sq : Square |
| App : Approach | Circ : Circle | Ga : Gate | Mkt : Market | Sta : Station |
| Arc : Arcade | Cir : Circus | Gt : Great | M : Mews | St : Street |
| Av : Avenue | Clo : Close | Grn : Green | Mt : Mount | Ter : Terrace |
| Bk : Back | Comn : Common | Gro : Grove | N : North | Up : Upper |
| Boulevd : Boulevard | Cotts : Cottages | Ho : House | Pal : Palace | Vs : Villas |
| Bri : Bridge | Ct : Court | Ind : Industrial | Pde : Parade | Wlk : Walk |
| B'way : Broadway | Cres : Crescent | Junct : Junction | Pk : Park | W : West |
| Bldgs : Buildings | Dri : Drive | La : Lane | Pas : Passage | Yd : Yard |
| Bus : Business | E : East | Lit : Little | Pl : Place | |
| Cen : Centre | Embkmt : Embankment | Lwr : Lower | Rd : Road | |
| Chu : Church | Est : Estate | Mnr : Manor | S : South | |

## POSTTOWN AND POSTAL LOCALITY ABBREVIATIONS

| | | | | |
|---|---|---|---|---|
| Asht : Ashtead | Esh : Esher | Hin W : Hinchley Wood | N Mald : New Malden | Th Dit : Thames Ditton |
| Bren : Brentford | Ewe : Ewell | Houn : Hounslow | Oxs : Oxshott | Twic : Twickenham |
| Cars : Carshalton | Felt : Feltham | Iswth : Isleworth | Rich : Richmond | W on T : Walton-on-Tha |
| Chess : Chessington | Ham : Ham | Kew : Kew | Sun : Sunbury-on-Thames | W Ewe : West Ewell |
| Clay : Claygate | Hamp : Hampton | King T : Kingston Upon | Surb : Surbiton | W Mol : West Molesey |
| Dit H : Ditton Hill | Hamp H : Hampton Hill | Thames | Sutt : Sutton | Whit : Whitton |
| E Mol : East Molesey | Hamp W : Hampton Wick | Lea : Leatherhead | Swan : Swanley | Wor Pk : Worcester Park |
| Eps : Epsom | Hanw : Hanworth | Mord : Morden | Tedd : Teddington | |

## INDEX TO STREETS

**A**bbey Ct. Hamp —4F **13**
Abbey Gdns. W6 —3H **5**
Abbey Wlk. W Mol —7G **13**
Abbotsbury Rd. Mord
—2K **23**
Abbotstone Rd. SW15 —7F **5**
Abbott Av. SW20 —5G **17**
Abbott Clo. Hamp —3D **12**
Abbottsmede Clo. Twic
—6A **8**
Abbotts Rd. Sutt —7H **23**
(in two parts)
Abbott's Tilt. W on T —7D **18**
Abingdon Rd. W8 —1K **5**
Abingdon Vs. W8 —1K **5**
Abinger Gdns. Iswth —1K **7**
Abinger Rd. W4 —1B **4**
Aboyne Dri. SW20 —6D **16**
Acacia Av. Bren —4C **2**
Acacia Av. Rich —6G **3**
Acacia Dri. Sutt —5K **23**
Acacia Rd. Hamp —3F **13**
A.C. Court. Th Dit —3B **20**
Acfold Rd. SW6 —5K **5**
Ackmar Rd. SW6 —5K **5**
Acorn Clo. Hamp —3G **13**
Acre Rd. King T —1F **15**
Acton La. W4 & W3 —1K **3**
(in three parts)
Acuba Rd. SW18 —6K **11**
Adams Clo. Surb —3G **21**
Adams Wlk. King T —6F **15**
*Adam Wlk. SW6 —4F 5*
*(off Crabtree La.)*
Addington Ct. SW14 —7A **4**
Addison Bri. Pl. W14 —1J **5**
Addison Gdns. Surb —6G **21**
Addison Gro. W4 —1B **4**
Addison Rd. W14 —1J **5**
Addison Rd. Tedd —3C **14**
*Addison Ter. W4 —1K 3*
*(off Chiswick Rd.)*
Adecroft Way. W Mol
—7H **13**

Adela Av. N Mald —2E **22**
Adelaide Rd. SW18 —2K **11**
Adelaide Rd. Rich —1G **9**
Adelaide Rd. Surb —2F **21**
Adelaide Rd. Tedd —3A **14**
Adelaide Rd. W on T —7A **18**
Adelaide Ter. Bren —2E **2**
Adelphi Ct. W4 —3A **4**
Adeney Clo. W6 —3G **5**
Adie Rd. W6 —1F **5**
Admark Ho. Eps —4J **27**
Admiralty Rd. Tedd —3A **14**
Agar Clo. Surb —6G **21**
Agate Rd. W6 —1F **5**
Agates La. Asht —7E **26**
Ailsa Av. Twic —2B **8**
Ailsa Rd. Twic —2C **8**
*Aintree Est. SW6 —4H 5*
*(off Aintree St.)*
Aintree St. SW6 —4H **5**
Airedale Av. W4 —1C **4**
Airedale Av. S. W4 —2C **4**
Aisgill Av. W14 —2J **5**
Akehurst St. SW15 —3D **10**
Akerman Rd. Surb —3D **20**
Alan Rd. SW19 —2H **17**
Albany Clo. SW14 —1J **9**
Albany M. King T —2E **14**
Albany Pde. Bren —3F **3**
Albany Pk. Rd. King T
—3E **14**
Albany Pas. Rich —2F **9**
Albany Pl. Bren —3E **2**
Albany Rd. SW19 —2K **17**
Albany Rd. Bren —3F **3**
Albany Rd. N Mald —1A **22**
Albany Rd. Rich —2G **9**
Albemarle. SW19 —6G **11**
Albemarle Gdns. N Mald
—1A **22**
Albemarle Av. Twic —5E **6**
Albert Dri. SW19 —6H **11**
Albert Rd. SW19 —2J **17**
Albert Rd. Asht —7G **27**
Albert Rd. Hamp —2H **13**

Albert Rd. Houn —1F **7**
Albert Rd. King T —6G **15**
Albert Rd. N Mald —1C **22**
Albert Rd. Rich —2F **9**
Albert Rd. Tedd —3A **14**
Albert Rd. Twic —5A **8**
Albion Gdns. W6 —1E **4**
Albion M. W6 —1E **4**
Albion Pl. W6 —1E **4**
Albion Rd. Houn —1F **7**
Albion Rd. King T —5K **15**
Albion Rd. Twic —5K **7**
Albury Av. Iswth —4A **2**
Albury Clo. Hamp —3G **13**
Albury Rd. Chess —2F **25**
Alcorn Clo. Sutt —6K **23**
Aldensley Rd. W6 —1E **4**
Alderbury Rd. SW13 —3D **4**
Alder Lodge. SW6 —5G **5**
Alderman Judge Mall. King T
—6F **15**
Aldersbrook Dri. King T
—3G **15**
Alders Gro. E Mol —2J **19**
Alders, The. Felt —1D **12**
Alderville Rd. SW6 —6J **5**
Aldridge Rise. N Mald
—4B **22**
Alexa Ct. W8 —1K **5**
Alexander Clo. Twic —6A **8**
Alexander Godley Clo. Asht
—7G **27**
Alexandra Av. W4 —4A **4**
Alexandra Av. Sutt —7K **23**
Alexandra Clo. W on T
—6A **18**
Alexandra Dri. Surb —6H **21**
Alexandra Gdns. W4 —4B **4**
Alexandra M. SW19 —3J **17**
Alexandra Rd. SW14 —7A **4**
Alexandra Rd. SW19 —3J **17**
Alexandra Rd. Bren —3G **3**
Alexandra Rd. King T —4H **15**
Alexandra Rd. Rich —6G **3**

Alexandra Rd. Th Dit —2A **20**
Alexandra Rd. Twic —3D **8**
Alexandra Sq. Mord —2K **23**
Alfred La. Felt —6B **6**
Alfred Rd. King T —7F **15**
Alfreton Clo. SW19 —7G **11**
Alfriston. Surb —3G **21**
Alfriston Clo. Surb —2G **21**
Algar Clo. Iswth —7B **2**
Algar Rd. Iswth —7B **2**
Alice Ct. SW15 —1J **11**
*Alice Gilliatt Ct. W14 —3J 5*
*(off Star Rd.)*
Alice M. Tedd —2A **14**
Alice Way. Houn —1G **7**
Alkerden Rd. W4 —2B **4**
Allan Clo. N Mald —2A **22**
Allbrook Clo. Tedd —2K **13**
Allen Clo. Sun —5A **12**
Allen Rd. Sun —5A **12**
Allestree Rd. SW6 —4H **5**
Allgood Clo. Mord —3G **23**
Allington Clo. SW19 —2G **17**
All Saints Dri. SW18 —2K **11**
Alma Ho. Bren —3F **3**
Alma Rd. Esh —5K **19**
Alma Ter. W8 —1K **5**
Almer Rd. SW20 —4D **16**
Almond Gro. Bren —4C **2**
Almshouse La. Chess —5E **24**
Alpha Rd. Surb —3G **21**
Alpha Rd. Tedd —2J **13**
Alpine Av. Surb —6K **21**
Alpine Rd. W on T —4A **18**
Alric Av. N Mald —7B **16**
Alsom Av. Wor Pk —7D **22**
Alston Clo. Surb —4C **20**
Alt Gro. SW19 —4J **17**
Alton Clo. Iswth —4A **2**
Alton Gdns. Twic —4J **8**
Alton Rd. SW15 —5D **10**
Alton Rd. Rich —1F **9**
Alverstone Av. SW19 —6K **11**
Alverstone Rd. N Mald
—1C **22**

Alway Av. Eps —2K **25**
Alwyn Av. W4 —2A **4**
Alwyne Rd. SW19 —5J **17**
Amalgamated Dri. Bren —
Amberley Way. Houn —
Amberley Way. Mord —
Amberwood Rise. N Mald

Ambleside Av. W on T

Amerland Rd. SW18 —
Amesbury Clo. Wor Pk
Amesbury Rd. Felt —6C
Amhurst Gdns. Iswth —
Amis Av. Eps —3J **25**
Amity Gro. SW20 —5E
Amor Rd. W6 —1F **5**
Amyand Cotts. Twic —
Amyand La. Twic —4C **8**
Amyand Pk. Gdns. Twic

Amyand Pk. Rd. Twic —
Ancaster Cres. N Mald
Anchorage Clo. SW19
Ancill Clo. W6 —3G **5**
Anderson Clo. Eps —1J
Anderson Pl. Houn —1G
Andover Rd. Twic —5J
Andrews Clo. Wor Pk
Angelfield. Houn —2G **7**
Angel Rd. Th Dit —4B **2**
Angel Wlk. W6 —1F **5**
Anglers Clo. Rich —1D
Anglesea Rd. King T —
Angus Clo. Chess —2H
Anlaby Rd. Tedd —2K **1**
Annandale Rd. W4 —2K
Anne Boleyn's Wlk. King
Anne Case M. N Mald

Beechwood Av. Sun —3A **12**
Beechwood Clo. Surb
—4D **20**
Beechwood Ct. W4 —3A **4**
Beechwood Ct. Sun —3A **12**
Beechwood Gro. Surb
—4D **20**
Beecot La. W on T —6B **18**
Beeston Way. Felt —3B **6**
Begonia Pl. Hamp —3F **13**
Belcombe Av. Wor Pk
—5F **23**
Beldham Gdns. W Mol
—6G **13**
Belgrade Rd. Hamp —5G **13**
Belgrave Ct. W4 —2K **3**
Belgrave Cres. Sun —5A **12**
Belgrave Rd. SW13 —4C **4**
Belgrave Rd. Houn —1E **6**
Belgrave Rd. Sun —5A **12**
Belgravia M. King T —1E **20**
Bellamy Clo. W14 —2J **5**
Bell Dri. SW18 —4H **11**
Bellevue Rd. SW13 —6D **4**
Bellevue Rd. King T —7F **15**
Bell Junct. Houn —1G **7**
Bell La. Twic —5B **8**
Bell Rd. E Mol —2J **19**
Bell Rd. Houn —1G **7**
Bells All. SW6 —6K **5**
Belmont Av. N Mald —2D **22**
Belmont Rd. W4 —1A **4**
Belmont Rd. W4 —1A **4**
Belmont Rd. Twic —6J **7**
Belmont Ter. W4 —1A **4**
Beloe Clo. SW15 —1D **10**
Belsize Av. W13 —1C **2**
Beltane Dri. SW19 —7G **11**
Beltran Rd. SW6 —6K **5**
Belvedere Av. SW19 —2H **17**
Belvedere Clo. Tedd —2K **13**
Belvedere Dri. SW19 —2H **17**
Belvedere Gdns. W Mol
—2E **18**
Belvedere Gro. SW19 —2H **17**
Belvedere Sq. SW19 —2H **17**
Bemish Rd. SW15 —1G **5**
Bench, The. Rich —7D **8**
Bendemeer Rd. SW15 —7G **5**
Benham Gdns. Houn —2E **6**
Bennett Clo. Hamp —5D **14**
Bennett St. W4 —3B **4**
Benn's All. Hamp —6G **13**
Benns Wlk. Rich —1F **9**
Bensbury Clo. SW15 —4E **10**
Benson Rd. Houn —1F **7**
Bentall Cen., The. King T
—5E **14**
Beresford Av. Surb —5J **21**
Beresford Av. Twic —3D **8**
Beresford Gdns. Houn —2E **6**
Beresford Rd. King T —5G **15**
Beresford Rd. N Mald
—1K **21**
Berestede Rd. W6 —2C **4**
Berghem M. W14 —1G **5**
Berkeley Clo. Bren —3B **2**
Berkeley Clo. King T —4F **15**
Berkeley Ct. Asht —7G **27**
Berkeley Ct. Surb —4E **20**
Berkeley Dri. W Mol —7E **12**
Berkeley Gdns. Clay —3B **24**
Berkeley Ho. Bren —3E **2**
(off Albany Rd.)
Berkeley Pl. SW19 —3G **17**
Berkeley Rd. SW13 —5D **4**
Bernard Gdns. SW19 —2J **17**
Berry Ct. Houn —2E **6**
Berrylands. SW20 —1F **23**
Berrylands. Surb —3G **21**
Berrylands Rd. Surb —3G **21**
Berry Meade. Asht —6G **27**
Bertram Cotts. SW19 —4K **17**
Bertram Rd. King T —4H **15**
Berwyn Rd. Rich —1J **9**
Beryl Rd. W6 —2G **5**

Berystede. King T —4J **15**
Bessborough Rd. SW15
—5D **10**
Betley Ct. W on T —7A **18**
Bettridge Rd. SW6 —6J **5**
Betts Way. Surb —5C **20**
Beulah Rd. SW19 —4J **17**
Beverley Av. SW20 —5C **16**
Beverley Av. Houn —1E **6**
Beverley Clo. SW13 —6D **4**
Beverley Clo. Chess —1D **24**
Beverley Ct. W4 —2K **3**
Beverley Ct. Houn —1E **6**
—5C **16**
Beverley Gdns. SW13 —7C **4**
Beverley Gdns. Wor Pk
—5D **22**
Beverley La. SW15 —7C **10**
Beverley La. King T —4B **16**
Beverley Path. SW13 —6C **4**
Beverley Rd. SW13 —7C **4**
Beverley Rd. W4 —2C **4**
Beverley Rd. King T —5D **14**
Beverley Rd. N Mald —1D **22**
Beverley Rd. Wor Pk —6F **23**
Beverley Way. N Mald & SW20
—5C **16**
Bexhill Clo. Felt —6D **6**
Bexhill Rd. SW14 —7K **3**
Bicester Rd. Rich —7H **3**
Bideford Clo. Felt —7E **6**
Biggs Row. SW15 —7G **5**
Billockby Clo. Chess —3G **25**
Binns Rd. W4 —2B **4**
Birch Clo. Bren —4C **2**
Birch Clo. Tedd —2B **14**
Birches, The. Houn —4E **6**
Birchington Rd. Surb —4G **21**
Birch Rd. Felt —2C **12**
Birchwood Clo. Mord —1K **23**
Birchwood Gro. Hamp
—3F **13**
Bird Wlk. Twic —5E **6**
Birdwood Clo. Tedd —1K **13**
Birkbeck Rd. W5 —1D **2**
Birkenhead Av. King T
—6G **15**
Biscay Rd. W6 —2G **5**
Bishop Clo. W4 —2K **3**
Bishop Fox Way. W Mol
—1E **18**
Bishop King's Rd. W14
—1H **5**
Bishop's Av. SW6 —6G **5**
Bishops Clo. Rich —7E **8**
Bishop's Clo. Sutt —7K **23**
Bishops Ct. Rich —7F **3**
Bishop's Gro. Hamp —1E **12**
Bishop's Hall. King T —6E **14**
Bishop's Mans. SW6 —5H **5**
(in two parts)
Bishop's Pk. Rd. SW6 —6G **5**
Bishop's Rd. SW6 —5H **5**
Bisley Clo. Wor Pk —5F **23**
Bison Ct. Felt —4A **6**
Bittoms, The. King T —7E **14**
Blackford's Path. SW15
—4D **10**
Black Lion La. W6 —1D **4**
Black Lion M. W6 —1D **4**
Blackmore's Gro. Tedd
—3B **14**
Blacksmith Clo. Asht —7G **27**
Blacks Rd. W6 —2F **5**
Blade M. SW15 —1J **11**
Blades Ct. SW15 —1J **11**
Blagdon Rd. N Mald —1C **22**
Blagdon Wlk. Tedd —3D **14**
Blair Av. Esh —6H **19**
Blakeden Dri. Clay —3A **24**
Blake Gdns. SW6 —5K **5**
Blakeney Clo. Eps —7K **25**
Blakes Av. N Mald —2C **22**
Blakes La. N Mald —2C **22**
Blakesley Wlk. SW20 —6J **17**
Blakes Ter. N Mald —2D **22**

Blakewood Clo. Felt —1B **12**
Blandford Av. Twic —5G **7**
Blandford Rd. Tedd —2J **13**
Blenheim Clo. SW20 —7F **17**
Blenheim Gdns. King T
—4J **15**
Blenheim Ho. Houn —1F **7**
Blenheim Rd. SW20 —7F **17**
Blenheim Rd. W4 —1B **4**
Blenheim Rd. Sutt —7K **23**
Blincoe Clo. SW19 —6G **11**
Blondin Av. W5 —1D **2**
Bloomfield Rd. King T
—7F **15**
Bloom Pk. Rd. SW6 —4J **5**
Bloomsbury Clo. Eps —6K **25**
Bloxham Cres. Hamp —4E **12**
Blue Anchor All. Rich —1F **9**
Bluefield Clo. Hamp —2F **13**
Blyth Clo. Twic —3A **8**
Blythe Rd. W14 —1G **5**
Boars Head Yd. Bren —4E **2**
Bockhampton Rd. King T
—4G **15**
Boddicott Clo. SW19 —6H **11**
Bodley Clo. N Mald —2B **22**
Bodley Rd. N Mald —3A **22**
Bodmin St. SW18 —5K **11**
Bodnant Gdns. SW20
—7D **16**
Boileau Rd. SW13 —4D **4**
Boleyn Dri. W Mol —7E **12**
Bollo La. W3 & W4 —1J **3**
Bolney Way. Felt —7D **6**
Bolton Clo. Chess —3E **24**
Bolton Gdns. SW5 —2K **5**
Bolton Gdns. Tedd —3B **14**
Bolton Rd. W4 —4K **3**
Bolton Rd. Chess —3E **24**
Bond Rd. Surb —6G **21**
Bond St. W4 —1A **4**
Bonner Hill Rd. King T
—6G **15**
Bonser Rd. Twic —6A **8**
Bordesley Rd. Mord —1K **23**
Bordon Wlk. SW15 —4D **10**
Borland Rd. Tedd —4C **14**
Borneo St. SW15 —7H **5**
Borough Rd. Iswth —5A **2**
Borough Rd. King T —5H **15**
Boscombe Rd. SW19 —5K **17**
Boscombe Rd. Wor Pk
—5F **23**
Boston Gdns. W4 —3B **4**
Boston Gdns. W7 —1B **2**
Boston Gdns. Bren —1B **2**
Boston Mnr. Rd. Bren —1B **2**
Boston Pde. W7 —1B **2**
Boston Rd. W7 —1B **2**
Boston Vale. W7 —1B **2**
Bothwell St. W6 —3G **5**
Botsford Rd. SW20 —6H **17**
Boucher Clo. Tedd —2A **14**
Boulton Ho. Bren —2F **3**
Boundaries Rd. Felt —5B **6**
Boundary Clo. King T —7J **15**
Bourne Ct. W4 —3K **3**
Bourne Gro. Asht —7E **26**
Bournemouth Rd. SW19
—5K **17**
Bourne Pl. W4 —2A **4**
Bourne Way. Eps —1K **25**
Bowderdean St. SW6 —5H **5**
Bowes Rd. W on T —6A **18**
Bowfell Rd. W6 —3F **5**
Bow La. Mord —3H **23**
Bowling Grn. Clo. SW15
—4E **10**
Bowman M. SW18 —5J **11**
Bowness Cres. SW15 —2B **16**
Bowness Dri. Houn —1D **6**
Bowyers Clo. Asht —7G **27**
Boyd Clo. King T —4H **15**
Boyle Farm Rd. Th Dit
—3B **20**

Brackenbury Rd. W6 —1E **4**
Bracken Clo. Twic —4F **7**
Bracken End. Iswth —2J **7**
Bracken Gdns. SW13 —6D **4**
Bracken Path. Eps —2J **27**
Brackley Rd. W4 —2B **4**
Brackley Ter. W4 —2B **4**
Bradbourne St. SW6 —6K **5**
Braddon Rd. Rich —7G **3**
Bradmore Pk. Rd. W6 —1E **4**
Bradstone Rd. Rich —5G **3**
Braemar Av. SW19 —6K **11**
Braemar Rd. Bren —3E **2**
Braemar Rd. Wor Pk —7E **22**
Braeside Av. SW19 —5H **17**
Braid Clo. Felt —6E **6**
Brainton Av. Felt —4A **6**
Bramber Ct. W5 —1F **3**
Bramber Ct. Bren —1F **3**
Bramber Rd. W14 —3J **5**
Bramble La. Hamp —3E **12**
Brambles Clo. Iswth —4C **2**
Bramble Wlk. Eps —3J **27**
Bramcote Av. SW15 —1E **10**
Bramham Gdns. Chess
—1E **24**
Bramley Clo. Twic —3H **7**
Bramley Rd. W5 —1D **2**
Bramley Way. Asht —6G **27**
Bramley Way. Houn —2E **6**
Bramshaw Rise. N Mald
—3B **22**
Bramwell Clo. Sun —6C **12**
Brandlehow Rd. SW15
—1J **11**
Branksea St. SW6 —4H **5**
Branksome Clo. W on T
—6C **18**
Branksome Rd. SW19
—5K **17**
Branksome Way. N Mald
—5K **15**
Bransby Rd. Chess —3F **25**
Branstone Rd. Rich —5G **3**
Brantwood Av. Iswth —3B **8**
Brathway Rd. SW18 —4K **11**
Braybourne Dri. Iswth —4A **2**
Braycourt Av. W on T
—4A **18**
Breamore Clo. SW15 —5D **10**
Breamwater Gdns. Rich
—7C **8**
Breasley Clo. SW15 —1F **11**
Brecon Clo. Wor Pk —6F **23**
Brecon Rd. W6 —3G **5**
Brende Gdns. W Mol —1G **19**
Brentford Bus. Cen. Bren
—4D **2**
Brentford Ho. Twic —4C **8**
Brent Lea. Bren —4D **2**
Brent Rd. Bren —3D **2**
Brent Side. Bren —3D **2**
Brentside Executive Pk. Bren
—3D **2**
Brentwater Bus. Pk. Bren
—4D **2**
Brent Way. Bren —4E **2**
Brentwick Gdns. Bren —1F **3**
Brettgrave. Eps —6K **25**
Brett Ho. Clo. SW19 —4G **11**
Brewers La. Rich —2E **8**
Brewery La. Twic —4A **8**
Brewery M. Bus. Cen. Iswth
—7A **2**
Brewhouse St. SW15 —7H **5**
Briane Rd. Eps —6K **25**
Briar Clo. Hamp —2E **12**
Briar Clo. Iswth —2A **8**
Briar Ct. Sutt —7F **23**
Briar Rd. Twic —5K **7**
Briar Wlk. SW15 —1E **10**
Brick Farm Clo. Rich —5J **3**
Brickfield Clo. Bren —4D **2**
Bridge Av. W6 —1F **5**
Bridge Clo. Tedd —1A **14**
Bridge Gdns. E Mol —1J **19**

Bridgeman Rd. Tedd —3⬚
Bridgepark. SW18 —2K⬚
Bridge Rd. Chess —2F⬚
Bridge Rd. E Mol —1J **1**
Bridge Rd. Iswth —1J **7**
Bridge Rd. Twic —3C **8**
Bridges Pl. SW6 —5J **5**
Bridges Rd. SW19 —3K⬚
Bridges Rd. M. SW19 —⬚
Bridge St. W4 —1A **4**
Bridge St. Rich —2E **8**
Bridge View. W6 —2F **5**
Bridge Way. Twic —4H⬚
Bridge Wharf Rd. Iswth⬚
Bridge Wharf Rd. Iswth⬚
Bridgewood Rd. Wor Pk⬚
Bridle Clo. Eps —2K **25**
Bridle Clo. King T —1E⬚
Bridle Clo. Sun —7A **12**
Bridle Rd. Clay —3C **24**
Brighton Rd. Surb —3D⬚
Brinkley Rd. Wor Pk —⬚
Brinsworth Clo. Twic —⬚
Brinsworth Ho. Twic —⬚
Brisbane Av. SW19 —5⬚
Bristol Gdns. SW15 —4⬚
Bristow Rd. Houn —1H⬚
Britannia La. Twic —4H⬚
Britannia Rd. SW6 —4K⬚
Britannia Rd. Surb —4G⬚
British Gro. W4 —2C **4**
British Gro. W6 —2C **4**
British Gro. S. W6 —2D⬚
Broad Clo. W on T —7D⬚
Broadfields. E Mol —3K⬚
Broadhurst. Asht —5F **2**
Broadhurst Clo. Rich —⬚
Broadlands Ct. Rich —⬚
(off Kew Gdns. Rd.)
Broadlands, The. Felt —⬚
Broadlands Way. N Mald⬚
Broad La. Hamp —4E **1**
Broad Mead. Asht —7G⬚
Broadmead Av. Wor Pk⬚
Broadmead Clo. Hamp⬚
Broadoaks. Surb —6J **2**
Broad St. Tedd —3A **14**
Broad Wlk. Rich —4G **3**
Broad Wlk., The. E Mol⬚
Broadway. Surb —5J **21**
Broadway Arc. W6 —5J⬚
(off Hammersmith B'w⬚
Broadway Av. Twic —3⬚
Broadway Ct. SW19 —3⬚
Broadway Pl. SW19 —3⬚
Broadway, The. SW13 —⬚
Broadway, The. SW19⬚
Broadway, The. Th Dit⬚
Brockenhurst. W Mol —⬚
Brockenhurst Av. Wor P⬚
Brockham Clo. SW19 —⬚
Brocks Dri. Sutt —7H **2**
Brockshot Clo. Bren —⬚
Brompton Clo. Houn —⬚
Brompton Pk. Cres. SW⬚
Bronsart Rd. SW6 —4H⬚
Bronson Rd. SW20 —7E⬚
Brook Clo. SW20 —7E⬚
Brookers Clo. Asht —⬚
Brookfield Gdns. Clay —⬚
Brook Gdns. SW13 —3⬚
Brook Gdns. King T —⬚
Brook Grn. W6 —1G **5**
Brooklands Av. SW19 —⬚

nds Rd. Th Dit
　　　　—5A 20
a. N. Bren —2E 2
o parts)
a. Trading Cen. Bren
　　　　—2E 2
as. SW6 —4K 5
ld. Surb —6F 21
ld. Twic —3B 8
ld. S. Bren —3E 2
de Clo. Felt —7A 6
de Cres. Wor Pk
　　　　—5D 22
La. W4 —3H 3
Rd. W4 —2H 3
t. King T —6F 15
le Rd. SW6 —4J 5
Vay. Lea —7B 26
ood Av. SW13 —6C 4
ood Rd. SW18 —5J 11
Clo. Tedd —4E 14
Rd. Hamp —4E 12
eld. Sun —5A 8
eld Rd. Rich —5G 3
eld Rd. Surb —6G 21
eld Rd. Tedd —3D 14
all Rd. SW18 —2K 11
ouse La. SW6 —6K 5
ouse Rd. SW6 —6K 5
oan La. Sutt —6K 23
Lock. Tedd —3D 14
Pk. Tedd —4E 14
Rd. Tedd —2C 14
Water. Tedd —3D 14
Water W. Tedd
　　　　—2D 14
ton Av. Rich —7C 8
s La. Felt —6A 6
Bear Ct. Felt —1C 12
ig Av. Wor Pk
　　　　—5E 22
ng Clo. Hamp —1E 12
s Rd. Surb —4G 21
me Ho. SW6 —5K 5
arwood Rd.)
ld Rd. Eps —2K 25
Wlk. —4F 7
ick Clo. Th Dit
　　　　—5A 20
ick Clo. Twic —7J 7
ick Clo. W on T
　　　　—6B 18
ick Rd. King T
　　　　—5H 15
on Av. Twic —5G 7
s Clo. Eps —3K 27
ld Rd. SW18 —3K 11
ham Av. Felt —3A 6
ham Av. W Mol
　　　　—6G 13
ham Clo. Hamp
　　　　—2E 12
ham Gdns. W Mol
　　　　—6G 13
ham Rd. Hamp
　　　　—1E 12
ham Rd. King T
　　　　—1G 21
ham Rd. Rich —6E 8
d Rd. Chess —2G 25
ds Rd. Tedd —3D 14
d's Wharf. King T
　　　　—6E 14
d Way. Wor Pk
　　　　—5F 23
gh Av. SW20 —7H 17
s All. SW6 —3J 5
s Clo. Eps —3K 27
All. Twic —2D 8
. SW6 —6H 5
ll. SW14 —6A 4
y Clo. N Mald —6B 16
Clo. Bren —2D 2
shott Av. Rich —1J 9
Av. SW20 —5D 16
Rd. Rich —6G 3

Burford Ho. Bren —2F 3
Burford Rd. Bren —2F 3
Burford Rd. Sutt —6K 23
Burford Rd. Wor Pk —4C 22
Burgess Clo. Felt —1D 12
Burghley Av. N Mald —5A 16
Burghley Rd. SW19 —1G 17
Burke Clo. SW15 —1B 10
Burleigh Pl. SW15 —2G 11
Burleigh Rd. Sutt —5B 23
Burlington Av. Rich —5H 3
Burlington Gdns. W4 —2K 3
Burlington La. W4 —4K 3
Burlington Pl. SW6 —6H 5
Burlington Rd. SW6 —6H 5
Burlington Rd. W4 —2K 3
Burlington Rd. N Mald
　　　　—1C 22
Burnaby Cres. W4 —3K 3
Burnaby Gdns. W4 —3J 3
Burne Jones Ho. W14 —1H 5
(off N. End Rd.)
Burnell Av. Rich —2D 14
Burnet Gro. Eps —2K 27
Burney Av. Surb —2G 21
Burnfoot Av. SW6 —5H 5
Burnham Dri. Wor Pk
　　　　—6G 23
Burnham St. King T —5H 15
Burnham Way. W13 —1C 2
Burnside. Asht —7G 27
Burnside Clo. Twic —3B 8
Burnthwaite Rd. SW6 —4J 5
Burritt Rd. King T —6H 15
Burr Rd. SW18 —5H 11
Burstock Rd. SW15 —1H 11
Burston Rd. SW15 —5H 11
Burstow Rd. SW20 —5H 17
Burtenshaw Rd. Th Dit
　　　　—4B 20
Burton Clo. Chess —4E 24
Burton Rd. King T —4F 15
Burton's Rd. Hamp —1G 13
Burwood Clo. Surb —5H 21
Burwood Pk. Rd. W on T
　　　　—7A 18
Bury Gro. Mord —2K 23
Bush Cotts. SW18 —2K 11
Bushey Ct. SW20 —6E 16
Bushey La. Sutt —7K 23
Bushey Rd. SW20 —7E 16
Bushey Rd. Sutt —7K 23
Bushey Shaw. Asht —6D 26
Bush Rd. Rich —3G 3
Bushwood Rd. Rich —3H 3
Bushy Ct. King T —5D 14
(off Up. Teddington Rd.)
Bushy Pk. Gdns. Tedd
　　　　—2J 13
Bushy Pk. Rd. Tedd —4C 14
(in two parts)
Bute Av. Rich —6F 9
Bute Gdns. W6 —1G 5
Butterfield Clo. Twic —3A 8
Buttermere Clo. Mord
　　　　—3G 23
Buttermere Dri. SW15
　　　　—2H 11
Butterwick. W6 —1F 5
Butts Cotts. Felt —7D 6
Butts Cres. Felt —7F 7
Butts, The. Bren —3E 2
Butts, The. Sun —7B 12
Buxton Cres. Sutt —7H 23
Buxton Dri. N Mald —6A 16
Byatt Wlk. Hamp —3D 12
Bychurch End. Tedd —2A 14
Byeways. Twic —7G 7
Byeways, The. Surb —2H 21
Byfeld Gdns. SW13 —5D 4
Byfield Pas. Iswth —7B 2
Byfield Rd. Iswth —7B 2
Byron Av. N Mald —2D 22

Byron Clo. Hamp —1E 12
Byron Clo. W on T —5D 18
Byward Av. Felt —3B 6
Byways, The. Asht —7E 26

# Cadbury Clo. Iswth —5B 2
Cadman Ct. W4 —2J 3
(off Chaseley Dri.)
Cadmer Clo. N Mald —1B 22
Cadogan Clo. Tedd —2K 13
Cadogan Rd. Surb —2E 20
Caen Wood Rd. Asht —7D 26
Cairngorm Clo. Tedd —2B 14
Caithness Rd. W14 —1G 5
Caldbeck Av. Wor Pk —6E 22
California Rd. N Mald —7K 15
Calonne Rd. SW19 —3F 17
Calvary Gdns. SW15 —2J 11
Camac Rd. Twic —5J 7
Cambalt Rd. SW15 —2G 11
Camberley Av. SW20 —6E 16
Camberley Clo. Sutt —7G 23
Camborne Rd. SW18 —4K 11
Camborne Rd. Mord —2G 23
Cambourne Wlk. Rich —3E 8
Cambria Clo. Houn —1F 7
Cambria Ct. Felt —4A 6
Cambrian Rd. Rich —3G 9
Cambridge Av. N Mald
　　　　—7B 16
Cambridge Clo. SW20
　　　　—5E 16
Cambridge Clo. Houn —1D 6
Cambridge Cotts. Rich —3H 3
Cambridge Cres. Tedd
　　　　—2B 14
Cambridge Gdns. King T
　　　　—6H 15
Cambridge Gro. W6 —1E 4
Cambridge Gro. Rd. King T
　　　　—7H 15
Cambridge Pk. Twic —3D 8
Cambridge Pk. Ct. Twic
　　　　—4E 8
Cambridge Rd. SW13 —6C 4
Cambridge Rd. SW20
　　　　—5D 16
Cambridge Rd. Hamp —4E 12
Cambridge Rd. Houn —1D 6
Cambridge Rd. King T
　　　　—6G 15
Cambridge Rd. N Mald
　　　　—1B 22
Cambridge Rd. Rich —4H 3
Cambridge Rd. Tedd —1A 14
Cambridge Rd. Twic —3E 8
Cambridge Rd. W on T
　　　　—3A 18
Cambridge Rd. W Mol
　　　　—1E 18
Cambridge Rd. N. W4 —2J 3
Cambridge Rd. S. W4 —2J 3
Camborne Rd. Rich —3G 3
Camellia Pl. Twic —4G 7
Camelot Clo. SW19 —1K 17
Camm Gdns. King T —1G 21
Camm Gdns. Th Dit —4A 20
Campana Rd. SW6 —5K 5
Campbell Clo. Twic —5J 7
Campbell Rd. E Mol —7K 13
Campbell Rd. Twic —6J 7
Campden Clo. SW19 —6H 11
Campion Rd. SW15 —1F 11
Campion Rd. Iswth —5A 2
Camp Rd. SW19 —2E 16
Camp View. SW19 —2E 16
Camrose Av. Felt —1B 12
Camrose Clo. Mord —1K 23
Canbury Av. King T —5G 15
Canbury Pk. Rd. King T
　　　　—6G 15
Canbury Pas. King T —5E 14
Canbury Pl. King T —5F 15
Canford Gdns. N Mald
　　　　—3B 22

Cannizaro Rd. SW19 —3F 17
Cannon Clo. SW20 —1F 23
Cannon Clo. Hamp —3G 13
Cannon Hill La. SW20
　　　　—2G 23
Cannon Way. W Mol —1F 19
Canterbury Rd. Felt —6D 6
Capital Interchange Way. Bren
　　　　—2H 3
Cardiff Rd. W7 —1B 2
Cardigan Rd. SW13 —6D 4
Cardigan Rd. Rich —3F 9
Cardinal Av. King T —2F 15
Cardinal Av. Mord —3H 23
Cardinal Clo. Mord —3H 23
Cardinal Clo. Wor Pk —7D 22
Cardinal Cres. N Mald
　　　　—6K 15
Cardinal Dri. W on T —5C 18
Cardinal Pl. SW15 —1G 11
Cardinal Rd. Felt —5A 6
Cardinals Wlk. Hamp —4H 13
Cardington Sq. Houn —1C 6
Cardross St. W6 —1E 4
Carleton Clo. Esh —5J 19
Carlingford Rd. Mord —3G 23
Carlisle Clo. King T —5H 15
Carlisle Rd. King T —5H 15
Carlisle Rd. Hamp —4G 13
Carlton Av. Felt —3B 6
Carlton Clo. Chess —3E 24
Carlton Cres. Sutt —7H 23
Carlton Dri. SW15 —2G 11
Carlton Pk. Av. SW20
　　　　—6G 17
Carlton Rd. SW14 —7K 3
Carlton Rd. N Mald —6B 16
Carlton Rd. W on T —4A 18
Carlyle Clo. W Mol —6G 13
Carlyle Pl. SW15 —1G 11
Carlyle Rd. W5 —2D 2
Carmalt Gdns. SW15 —1F 11
Carnegie Clo. Surb —6G 21
Carnegie Pl. SW19 —7G 11
Carnforth Clo. Eps —3J 25
Carnwath Rd. SW6 —7K 5
Caroline Rd. SW19 —4J 17
Caroline Wlk. W6 —3H 5
Carpenters Ct. Twic —6K 7
Carrick Clo. Iswth —7B 2
Carrick Ga. Esh —7H 19
Carrington Av. Houn —2J 7
Carrington Rd. Rich —1H 9
Carslake Rd. SW15 —3F 11
Carters Clo. Wor Pk —5G 23
Carter's Yd. SW18 —2K 11
Carthew Rd. W6 —1E 4
Carville Cres. Bren —1F 3
Cassidy Rd. SW6 —4J 5
Cassilis Rd. Twic —2C 8
Castello Av. SW15 —2F 11
Castelnau. SW13 —5D 4
Castelnau Gdns. SW13 —3E 4
Castelnau Pl. SW13 —3E 4
Castelnau Row. SW13 —3E 4
Castlecombe Dri. SW19
　　　　—4G 11
Castlegate. Rich —7G 3
Castle Pl. W4 —1B 4
Castle Clo. Eps —4J 27
Castle Clo. Iswth —6A 2
Castle Row. W4 —2J 3
Castle St. King T —6F 15
Castle Way. SW19 —1B 12
Castle Way. Felt —1B 12
Castle Yd. Rich —2E 8
Catherine Gdns. Houn —1J 7
Catherine Rd. Surb —2E 20
Catherine Wheel Rd.
　　　　—4E 2

Cato's Hill. Esh —7G 19
Causeway Cen. Houn —1A 6
Causeway, The. SW18
Cannon Way. W Mol —1K 11
Causeway, The. SW19
　　　　—2F 17
Causeway, The. Chess
　　　　—1F 25
Causeway, The. Clay —4A 24
Causeway, The. Felt & Houn
　　　　—1A 6
Causeway, The. Tedd —3A 14
Cavalier Ct. Surb —5G 21
Cavalry Cres. Houn —1C 6
Cavendish Av. N Mald —2E 22
Cavendish Rd. W4 —5K 3
Cavendish Rd. N Mald
　　　　—1C 22
Cavendish Ter. Felt —6A 6
Caverleigh Way. Wor Pk
　　　　—5D 22
Cave Rd. Rich —1D 14
Caversham Av. Sutt —6H 23
Caversham Rd. King T
　　　　—6G 15
Cawdor Cres. W7 —1B 2
Caxton M. Bren —3E 2
Cecil Clo. Chess —1E 24
Cecil Rd. SW19 —4K 17
Cecil Rd. Houn —3G 7
Cedar Av. Twic —3G 7
Cedar Clo. SW15 —1A 16
Cedar Clo. E Mol —1K 19
Cedar Ct. SW19 —7G 11
Cedar Ct. Bren —3E 2
(off Boston Mnr. Rd.)
Cedarcroft Rd. Chess —1G 25
Cedar Heights. Rich —5F 9
Cedar Hill. Eps —5K 27
Cedarne Rd. SW6 —4K 5
Cedar Rd. E Mol —1K 19
Cedars Rd. SW13 —6D 4
Cedars Rd. W4 —3K 3
Cedars Rd. King T —5D 14
Cedars Rd. Mord —1K 23
Cedars, The. Tedd —3A 14
Cedar Ter. Rich —1F 9
Cedar Vista. Rich —6F 3
Celandine Rd. W on T
　　　　—7D 18
Centaurs Bus. Cen. Iswth
　　　　—3B 2
Central Av. Houn —1H 7
Central Av. W Mol —1E 18
Central Pde. Felt —4B 6
Central Rd. Mord —3K 23
Central Rd. Wor Pk —5D 22
Central School Path. SW14
　　　　—7K 3
Central Way. Felt —2A 6
Centre Ct. Shopping Cen.
　　　　SW19 —3J 17
Centre, The. Felt —4A 6
Century Ho. SW15 —1G 11
Ceylon Rd. W14 —1G 5
Chadwick Clo. Tedd —3B 14
Chaffers Mead. Asht —5G 27
Chaffinch Clo. Surb —7H 21
Chaldon Rd. SW6 —4H 5
Chalfont Way. W13 —1C 2
Chalford Clo. W Mol —1F 19
Chalgrove Av. Mord —4K 23
Chalkhill Rd. W6 —1G 5
Chalk La. Asht —7H 27
Chalk La. Eps —4K 27
Chalky La. Chess —6E 24
Challis Rd. Bren —2E 2
Challoner Cres. W14 —2J 5
Challoners Clo. E Mol —1J 5
Challoner St. W14 —2J 5
Chalmers Way. Felt —2A 6
Chamberlain Way. Felt
　　　　—1D 12

*A-Z Kingston & Richmond* 31

Chamberlain Way. Surb
—4F 21
Chancellor's Rd. W6 —2F 5
Chancellor's St. W6 —2F 5
Chancellors Wharf. W6 —2F 5
Chandler Clo. Hamp —5F 13
Chandos Av. W5 —1D 2
Chantree Grn. W4 —1K 3
Chantry Hurst. Eps —4K 27
Chantry Rd. Chess —2G 25
Chantry Sq. W8 —1K 5
Chapel Rd. Houn —1G 7
Chapel Rd. Twic —4C 8
Chapter Way. Hamp —1F 13
Chara Pl. W4 —3A 4
Chardin Rd. W4 —1B 4
Charles Rd. SW19 —5K 17
Charles St. SW13 —6B 4
Charleston Clo. Felt —7A 6
Charleville Mans. W14 —2H 5
(off Charleville Rd.)
Charleville Rd. W14 —2H 5
Charlotte M. W14 —1H 5
Charlotte Rd. SW13 —5C 4
Charlotte Sq. Rich —3G 9
Charlton Ho. Bren —3F 3
Charlwood Rd. SW15
—1G 11
Charlwood Ter. SW15
—1G 11
Charminster Av. SW19
—6K 17
Charminster Ct. Surb —4E 20
Charminster Rd. Wor Pk
—5G 23
Charmouth Ct. Rich —2G 9
Charnwood Av. SW19
—6K 17
Charnwood Clo. N Mald
—1B 22
Charter Ct. N Mald —7B 16
Charter Cres. Houn —1D 6
Charter Rd. King T —7J 15
Charter Sq. King T —6J 15
Chartfield Av. SW15 —2E 10
Chartfield Sq. SW15 —2G 11
Chartwell Pl. Sutt —7H 23
Chartwell Pl. Sutt —7J 23
Chase Ct. Iswth —6B 2
Chase Gdns. Twic —4J 7
Chaseley Dri. W4 —2J 3
Chaseside Av. SW20 —6H 17
Chase, The. SW20 —5H 17
Chase, The. Asht —7D 26
Chase, The. Sun —5A 12
Chatham Clo. Sutt —4J 23
Chatham Rd. King T —6H 15
Chatsworth Av. SW20
—5H 17
Chatsworth Clo. W4 —3K 3
Chatsworth Cres. Houn
—1J 7
Chatsworth Gdns. N Mald
—2C 22
Chatsworth Pl. Tedd —1B 14
Chatsworth Rd. W4 —3K 3
Chatterton Ct. Rich —6G 3
Chaucer Av. Rich —7H 3
Chaucer Gdns. Sutt —7K 23
Chaucer Ho. Sutt —7K 23
(off Chaucer Gdns.)
Chaucer Rd. Sutt —7K 23
Cheam Comn. Rd. Wor Pk
—6E 22
Cheeseman Clo. Hamp
—3D 12
Cheesemans Ter. W14 —2J 5
Chelmsford Clo. W6 —3G 5
Chelsea Clo. Hamp —2H 13
Chelsea Clo. Wor Pk —4D 22
Chelsea Gdns. W14 —7H 23
Cheltenham Av. Twic —4J 7
Cheltenham Clo. N Mald
—7K 15
Chelverton Rd. SW15
—1G 11

Chelwood Gdns. Rich —6H 3
Chelwood Gdns. Pas. Rich
—6H 3
Chepstow Clo. SW15 —2H 11
Cherimoya Gdns. W Mol
—7G 13
Cheriton Ct. W on T —5B 18
Cherry Clo. Mord —1H 23
Cherry Cres. Bren —4C 2
Cherry Garth. Bren —2E 2
Cherry Orchard. Asht —7J 27
Cherry Orchard Gdns. W Mol
—7E 12
Cherry Orchard Rd. W Mol
—7F 13
Cherry Way. Eps —3K 25
Cherry Wood Clo. King T
—4H 15
Cherrywood Ct. Tedd —2B 14
Cherrywood Dri. SW15
—2G 11
Cherrywood La. Mord
—1H 23
Chertsey Dri. Sutt —6H 23
Chertsey Rd. Twic —6G 7
Chervil Clo. Felt —7A 6
Cherwell Ct. Eps —1K 25
Chesfield Rd. King T —4F 15
Chesham Rd. King T —6H 15
Cheshire Gdns. Chess
—3E 24
Chesilton Rd. SW6 —5J 5
Chessington Clo. Eps —3K 25
Chessington Hall Gdns. Chess
—3E 24
Chessington Hill Pk. Chess
—2H 25
Chessington Pde. Chess
—3E 24
Chessington Rd. Eps —3H 25
Chesson Rd. W14 —3J 5
Chester Av. Rich —3G 9
Chester Av. Twic —5E 6
Chester Clo. SW15 —7E 4
Chester Clo. Sutt —6K 23
Chester Rd. SW19 —3F 17
Chesters, The. N Mald
—5B 16
Chesterton Clo. SW18
—2K 11
Chesterton Sq. W8 —1J 5
Chesterton Ter. King T
—6H 15
Chestnut All. SW6 —3J 5
Chestnut Av. SW14 —7A 4
Chestnut Av. Bren —1E 2
Chestnut Av. E Mol & Tedd
—7A 14
Chestnut Av. Esh —4J 19
Chestnut Av. Hamp —4F 13
Chestnut Ct. SW6 —3J 5
Chestnut Ct. Felt —2C 12
Chestnut Gro. Iswth —1B 8
Chestnut Gro. N Mald
—7A 16
Chestnut Rd. SW20 —6G 17
Chestnut Rd. King T —4F 15
Chestnut Rd. Twic —6K 7
Chestnuts, The. W on T
—6A 18
Chestnut Way. Felt —7A 6
Cheyne Av. Twic —5E 6
Cheyne Hill. Surb —1G 21
Chichester Clo. Hamp —3E 12
Chichester Way. Felt —4B 6
Chiddingstone St. SW6
—6K 5
Childerley St. SW6 —5H 5
Child's Pl. SW5 —1K 5
Child's St. SW5 —1K 5
Child's Wlk. SW5 —1K 5
Chillingworth Gdns. Twic
—7A 8

Chilmark Gdns. N Mald
—3D 22
Chiltern Av. Twic —5F 7
Chiltern Clo. Wor Pk —6F 23
Chiltern Dri. Surb —3H 21
Chilton Av. W5 —1E 2
Chilton Rd. Rich —7H 3
Chilworth Ct. SW19 —5G 11
Chipstead St. SW6 —5K 5
Chisholm Rd. Rich —3G 9
Chislehurst Rd. Rich —2F 9
Chiswick Bri. SW14 & W4
—6K 3
Chiswick Comn. Rd. W4
—1A 4
Chiswick High Rd. Bren & W4
(in two parts) —2H 3
Chiswick La. N. W4 —2B 4
Chiswick La. S. W4 —3C 4
Chiswick Mall. W4 & W6
—3C 4
Chiswick Plaza. W4 —3K 3
Chiswick Quay. W4 —5K 3
Chiswick Rd. W4 —1K 3
Chiswick Sq. W4 —3B 4
Chiswick Staithe. W4 —4J 3
Chiswick Ter. W4 —1K 3
Chiswick Village. W4 —3H 3
Chiswick Wharf. W4 —3C 4
Chobham Gdns. SW19
—6G 11
Cholmley Rd. Th Dit —3C 20
Cholmondeley Wlk. Rich
—2D 8
Christchurch Av. Tedd
—2B 14
Christchurch Gdns. Eps
—7J 25
Christ Chu. Mt. Eps —1J 27
Christchurch Pl. Eps —7J 25
Christ Chu. Rd. SW14 —2J 9
Christ Chu. Rd. Eps —1F 27
Christchurch Rd. Surb
—3G 21
Chudleigh Rd. Twic —3K 7
Chumleigh Wlk. Surb —1G 21
Church Av. SW14 —7A 4
Church Ct. Rich —2E 8
Churchfield Mans. SW6
(off New King's Rd.) —6J 5
Churchfield Rd. W on T
—4A 18
Churchfields. W Mol —7F 13
Churchfields Av. Felt —7E 6
Church Ga. SW6 —7H 5
Church Gro. King T —5D 14
Church Hill. SW19 —2J 17
Church Hill Rd. Surb —2F 21
Church Hill Rd. Sutt —7G 23
Church La. SW19 —5K 17
Church La. Chess —3G 25
Church La. Rich —5F 9
Church La. Tedd —2A 14
Church La. Th Dit —3A 20
Church La. Twic —6B 8
Church Meadow. Surb
—6D 20
Church Pas. Surb —2F 21
Church Pas. Twic —5C 8
Church Path. SW14 —7A 4
(in two parts)
Church Path. SW19 —6J 17
Church Path. W4 —1K 3
Church Rise. Chess —3G 25
Church Rd. SW13 —6C 4
Church Rd. SW19 —2H 17
(Wimbledon)
Church Rd. Asht —7E 26
Church Rd. Clay —3A 24
Church Rd. Felt —2C 12
Church Rd. Ham —1E 14
Church Rd. King T —6G 15
Church Rd. Rich —1F 9
Church Rd. Surb —5D 20
Church Rd. Tedd —1K 13

Church Rd. Wor Pk —5B 22
Church Side. Eps —2J 27
Church St. W4 —3C 4
Church St. Hamp —5H 13
Church St. Iswth —7C 2
Church St. King T —6E 14
Church St. Sun —7A 12
Church St. Twic —5B 8
Church Stretton Rd. Houn
—2H 7
Church Ter. Rich —2E 8
Church View. Rich —2F 9
Churchview Rd. Twic —5J 7
Church Wlk. SW13 —5D 4
Church Wlk. SW15 —2E 10
Church Wlk. SW20 —7F 17
Church Wlk. Bren —3D 2
(in two parts)
Church Wlk. Rich —2E 8
Church Wlk. Th Dit —3A 20
Churchward Ho. W14 —2J 5
(off Ivatt Pl.)
Churston Dri. Mord —2G 23
Circle Gdns. SW19 —6K 17
Clancarty Rd. SW6 —6K 5
Clare Cres. Lea —7B 26
Clare Lawn Av. SW14
—2A 10
Clare M. SW6 —4K 5
Claremont Av. N Mald
—2D 22
Claremont Av. Sun —5A 12
Claremont Gdns. Surb
—2F 21
Claremont Gro. W4 —4B 4
Claremont Rd. Surb —2F 21
Claremont Rd. Tedd —3A 14
Claremont Rd. Twic —4C 8
Clarence Av. N Mald —6K 15
Clarence La. SW15 —3B 10
Clarence Rd. SW19 —3K 17
Clarence Rd. W4 —2H 3
Clarence Rd. Rich —5G 3
Clarence Rd. Tedd —3A 14
Clarence St. King T —6E 14
Clarence St. Rich —1F 9
Clarence Ter. Houn —1G 7
Clarendon Ct. Rich —5G 3
Clarendon Cres. Twic —7J 7
Clarendon Dri. SW15 —1F 11
Clare Pl. SW15 —4C 10
Clare Rd. Houn —1E 6
Clare Wood. Lea —7C 26
Clarkes Av. Wor Pk —5G 23
Claudia Pl. SW19 —5H 11
Clavering Av. SW13 —3E 4
Clavering Clo. Twic —1B 14
Claverton. Asht —6F 27
Claxton Gro. W6 —2G 5
Claybrook Rd. W6 —3G 5
Claygate La. Esh —6B 20
Claygate La. Th Dit —5B 20
Clayhill. Surb —2H 21
Claymore Clo. Mord —4K 23
Clayponds Av. W5 & Bren
—1F 3
Clayponds Gdns. W5 —1E 2
Clayponds La. Bren —2F 3
Clayton Cres. Bren —2F 3
Clayton Rd. Chess —1D 24
Clayton Rd. Iswth —1K 7
Cleaveland Rd. Surb —2E 20
Clem Attlee Ct. SW6 —3J 5
Clem Attlee Est. SW6 —3J 5
Clement Rd. W4 —1A 4
Clement Rd. SW19 —2H 17
Clements Ct. Houn —1C 6
Clements Mead. Lea —7B 26
Clements Pl. Bren —2E 2
Clements Rd. W on T —6A 18
Clensham Ct. Sutt —6K 23
Clensham La. Sutt —6K 23
Clevedon Rd. King T —6H 15
Clevedon Rd. Twic —6D 8
Cleveland Av. SW20 —6J 17
Cleveland Av. W4 —1C 4

Cleveland Av. Hamp —
Cleveland Clo. W on T
Cleveland Gdns. SW13
Cleveland Gdns. Wor P
Cleveland Rise. Mord —
Cleveland Rd. SW13 —
Cleveland Rd. W4 —1K
Cleveland Rd. Iswth —
Cleveland Rd. N Mald
Cleveland Rd. Wor Pk
Cleves Rd. Rich —7D 8
Cleves Way. Hamp —4,
Clifden Rd. Bren —3E 1
Clifden Rd. Twic —5A
Clifford Av. SW14 —7J
Clifford Rd. Rich —6E
Clifton Av. Felt —7B 6
Clifton Gdns. W4 —1A
Clifton Pde. Felt —1B 1
Clifton Pk. Av. SW20 —
Clifton Rd. SW19 —3G
Clifton Rd. King T —4(
Clifton Rd. Tedd —1K
Clifton Wlk. W6 —1E 4
(off King St.)
Clinton Av. E Mol —1H
Clippesby Clo. Chess —
Clitherow Av. W7 —1B
Clitherow Ct. Bren —2
Clitherow Pas. Bren —
Clitherow Rd. Bren —2
Cliveden Rd. SW19 —!
Clive Rd. Twic —1B 14
Clockhouse Clo. SW19
Clock Tower Rd. Iswth
Cloister Clo. Tedd —2(
Cloisters Mall. King T -
Cloncurry St. SW6 —6
Clonmel Rd. SW6 —4J
Clonmel Rd. Tedd —1,
Clonmore St. SW18 —
Close, The. N Mald —6
Close, The. Rich —7J
Close, The. Sutt —4J 2
Cluny M. SW5 —1K 5
Clydesdale Gdns. Rich
Clymping Dene. Felt —
Coach Ho. La. SW19 —
Coalecroft Rd. SW15 —
Coates Wlk. Bren —2F
Cobbett Rd. Twic —5F
Cobblers Wlk. Hamp &
Cobb's Rd. Houn —1E
Cobham Av. N Mald —
Cobham Rd. King T —
Cochrane Rd. SW19 —
Cocks Cres. N Mald —
Colborne Way. Wor Pk
Coldstream Gdns. SW
Colebrook Clo. SW15
Cole Ct. Twic —4B 8
Coleherne M. SW10 —
Coleherne Rd. SW10 —
Colehill Gdns. SW6 —
Colehill La. SW6 —5H
Cole Pk. Gdns. Twic —
Cole Pk. Rd. Twic —3
Cole Pk. View. Twic —
Cole Rd. Twic —3B 8
Coleshill Rd. Tedd —3
Colet Gdns. W14 —1G
Colinette Rd. SW15 —
Coliston Pas. SW18 —
Coliston Rd. SW18 —
College Clo. Twic —5.

e Ct. W6 —2F 5
(Queen Caroline St.)
e Gdns. N Mald
—2C 22
e Rd. Iswth —5A 2
e Roundabout. King T
—7F 15
e Wlk. King T —7F 15
Clo. Eps —3H 25
wood Av. Surb
—5K 21
wood Clo. Twic —4F 7
wood Pl. W on T
—7A 18
wood Rd. Sutt —7K 23
s Path. Hamp —3E 12
All. Twic —5K 7
Ct. Eps —1K 25
Dri. W on T —7C 18
Rd. Twic —5K 7
al Av. Twic —2H 7
al Dri. W4 —1K 3
n Rd. SW14 —1K 9
bia Av. Wor Pk —4C 22
bia Sq. SW14 —1K 9
e Rd. W3 —1J 3
h Rd. W6 —3F 5
emartin Rd. SW18
—4H 11
ragh M. W14 —2H 5
ragh Rd. W14 —2H 5
erce Rd. Bren —4D 2
ondale. SW15 —7F 5
on La. Clay —4B 24
on Rd. SW13 —7E 4
on Rd. Clay —3B 24
on Side. Eps —4H 27
ass Hill. Rich —3E 8
on Cres. W4 —3K 3
on Cres. Chess —2F 25
on Rd. SW19 —3J 17
r Gdns. Sutt —6K 23
rs Clo. Tedd —4C 14
er Rd. SW6 —6K 5
on Clo. SW13 —4C 4
on Clo. SW20 —3G 23
on Rd. W4 —4A 4
on Rd. Twic —3G 7
on Way. Chess —7F 21
ught Av. SW14 —7K 3
ught Av. Houn —1D 6
ught Rd. N Mald
—1B 22
ught Rd. Rich —2G 9
ught Rd. Tedd —2J 14
d Dri. Wor Pk —5F 23
rt M. Iswth —2J 7
able Ct. W4 —2J 3
(Chaseley Dri.)
able Gdns. Iswth —2J 7
ance Rd. Twic —4G 7
nt Gdns. W5 —1D 2
ay Rd. SW20 —5F 17
ay Rd. Felt —2C 12
ay Rd. Houn —4E 6
ay Wlk. Hamp —3E 12
e Bank. King T
—5B 16
e Clo. Houn —1F 7
e Cres. Hamp —4E 12
e End. King T —4A 16
efield Clo. N Mald
—2B 22
e Gdns. SW20
—6D 16
e Gdns. N Mald
—1C 22
e Hill Glade. King T
—4B 16
e Hill Rd. King T
—4B 16
e Ho. Chase. N Mald
—5A 16
e La. SW20 —5C 16
be La. King T —5J 15

Coombe La. Flyover. King T
—5C 16
Coombe La. W. King T
—5J 15
Coombe Neville. King T
—4A 16
Coombe Pk. King T —2K 15
Coombe Ridings. King T
—2K 15
Coombe Rise. King T —5K 15
Coombe Rd. W4 —2B 4
Coombe Rd. Hamp —3E 12
Coombe Rd. N Mald —6B 16
Coombe Wlk. Sutt —7K 23
Coombewood Rd. King T
—2K 15
Coomer M. SW6 —3J 5
Coomer Pl. SW6 —3J 5
Coomer Rd. SW6 —3J 5
Coopers Ct. Iswth —6A 2
(off Woodlands Rd.)
Copenhagen Way. W on T
—7A 18
Cope Pl. W8 —1K 5
Copper Mill Dri. Iswth —6A 2
Coppice Clo. SW20 —7F 17
Coppice Dri. SW15 —3E 10
Coppsfield. W Mol —3F 13
Copse Glade. Surb —4E 20
Copse Hill. SW20 —5D 16
Copthall Gdns. Twic —5A 8
Coram Ho. W4 —2B 4
(off Wood St.)
Corban Rd. Houn —1F 7
Corbiere Ct. SW19 —3G 17
Corfe Clo. Asht —7D 26
Corkran Rd. Surb —4E 20
Corney Rd. W4 —3B 4
Cornish Ho. Bren —2G 3
Cornwall Av. Clay —4A 24
Cornwall Gro. W4 —2B 4
Cornwall Rd. Twic —4B 8
Coronation Wlk. Twic —5F 7
Corporate Dri. Felt —7A 6
Corporation Av. Houn —1D 6
Corscombe Clo. King T
—2K 15
Cortayne Ct. Twic —6K 7
Cortayne Rd. SW6 —6J 5
Cortis Rd. SW15 —3E 10
Cortis Ter. SW15 —3E 10
Cotman Clo. SW15 —3G 11
Cotsford Av. N Mald —2K 21
Cotswold Clo. King T —3K 15
Cotswold Rd. Hamp —3F 13
Cotswold Way. Wor Pk
—6F 23
Cottage Gro. Surb —3E 20
Cottenham Dri. SW20 —4E 16
Cottenham Pk. Rd. SW20
(in two parts) —5D 16
Cottenham Pl. SW20 —4E 16
Cotterill Rd. Surb —6F 21
Cottimore Av. W on T
—5A 18
Cottimore Cres. W on T
—4A 18
Cottimore La. W on T
—4A 18
Cottimore Ter. W on T
—4A 18
Cottington Rd. Felt —1C 12
Couchmore Av. Esh —6K 19
Country Way. Felt —3A 12
County Pde. Bren —4E 2
Court Clo. Twic —6J 7
Court Clo. Av. Twic —7G 7
Court Cres. Chess —3E 24
Courtenay Rd. Wor Pk
—7F 23
Court Farm Gdns. Eps
—7K 25
Courthope Rd. SW19 —2H 17
Courthope Vs. SW19 —4H 17
Court Ho. Mans. Eps —1K 27

Courtlands. Rich —2H 9
Courtlands Av. Hamp —3E 12
Courtlands Av. Rich —5J 3
Courtlands Rd. Surb —4H 21
Court La. Eps —2K 27
Court Way. Twic —4A 8
Coutts Av. Chess —2F 25
Coval Gdns. SW14 —1J 9
Coval La. SW14 —1J 9
Coval Pas. SW14 —1K 9
Coval Rd. SW14 —1K 9
Coverts Rd. Clay —4A 24
Cowleaze Rd. King T —5F 15
Cowley Rd. SW14 —7B 4
Cowper Rd. King T —2G 15
Cox Ho. W6 —3H 5
(off Field Rd.)
Cox La. Chess —1G 25
Cox La. Eps —2J 25
Coxwold Path. Chess —4F 25
Crabtree La. SW6 —4F 5
(in two parts)
Craddocks Av. Asht —6F 27
Craddocks Pde. Asht —6F 27
(in two parts)
Craig Rd. Rich —1D 14
Crammond Clo. W6 —3H 5
Cranborne Av. Surb —7H 21
Cranbrook Ct. Bren —3E 2
(off Somerset Rd.)
Cranbrook Dri. Esh —5H 19
Cranbrook Dri. Twic —5G 7
Cranbrook Rd. SW19 —4H 17
Cranbrook Rd. W4 —2B 4
Cranbrook Rd. Houn —1E 6
Crane Av. Iswth —2B 8
Cranebrook. Twic —6H 7
Crane Ct. Eps —1K 25
Craneford Clo. Twic —4A 8
Crane Ho. Felt —7F 7
Crane Mead Ct. Twic —4A 8
Crane Pk. Rd. Twic —6G 7
Crane Rd. Twic —5K 7
Cranes Dri. Surb —1G 21
Cranes Pk. Surb —1F 21
Cranes Pk. Av. Surb —1F 21
Cranes Pk. Cres. Surb
—1G 21
Crane Way. Twic —4H 7
Cranford Clo. SW20 —4E 16
Cranleigh Gdns. King T
—3G 15
Cranleigh Gdns. Sutt —6K 23
Cranleigh Rd. SW19 —7H 17
Cranleigh Rd. Esh —5H 19
Cranmer Av. W13 —1C 2
Cranmer Clo. Mord —3G 23
Cranmer Rd. Hamp —2G 13
Cranmer Rd. King T —2F 15
Craven Gdns. SW19 —2K 17
Craven Rd. King T —5G 15
Cray Av. Asht —5F 27
Crayke Hill. Chess —4H 27
Crediton Way. Clay —2B 24
Creek Rd. E Mol —1K 19
Crefeld Clo. W6 —3H 5
Creighton Rd. W5 —1E 2
Crescent Ct. Surb —2E 20
Crescent Gdns. SW19
—7K 17
Crescent Rd. SW20 —5G 17
Crescent Rd. King T —4H 15
Crescent Stables. SW15
—2H 11
Crescent, The. SW13 —6D 4
Crescent, The. SW19 —7K 17
Crescent, The. Eps —3H 27
(in two parts)
Crescent, The. N Mald
—6A 16
Crescent, The. Surb —2F 21
Crescent, The. W Mol —1F 19
Cresford Rd. SW6 —5K 5
Cressage Ho. Bren —3F 3
(off Ealing Rd.)

Cresswell Rd. Felt —7D 6
Cresswell Rd. Twic —3E 8
Creston Way. Wor Pk
—5G 23
Crest, The. Surb —2H 21
Crestway. SW15 —3D 10
Crestwood Way. Houn —2E 6
Cricketers Clo. Chess —1E 24
Crieff Ct. Tedd —4D 14
Crispen Rd. Felt —1D 12
Crispin Clo. Asht —6G 27
Crisp Rd. W6 —2F 5
Cristowe Rd. SW6 —6J 5
Crofters Clo. Iswth —2J 7
Crofton. Asht —7H 27
Crofton Av. W4 —4A 4
Crofton Av. W on T —7B 18
Crofton Ter. Rich —1G 9
Croftway. Rich —7C 8
Cromer Vs. Rd. SW18
—3J 11
Cromford Rd. SW18 —2K 11
Cromford Way. N Mald
—6A 16
Cromwell Av. W6 —2E 4
Cromwell Av. N Mald —2C 22
Cromwell Clo. W on T
—5A 18
Cromwell Cres. SW5 —1K 5
Cromwell Pl. SW14 —7K 3
Cromwell Rd. SW5 & SW7
—1K 5
Cromwell Rd. SW19 —2K 17
Cromwell Rd. Felt —5A 6
Cromwell Rd. Houn —1F 7
Cromwell Rd. King T —5F 15
Cromwell Rd. Tedd —3B 14
Cromwell Rd. W on T
—5A 18
Cromwell Rd. Wor Pk
—7A 22
Crondace Rd. SW6 —5K 5
Crondace Rd. SW6 —5K 5
Crookham Rd. SW6 —5J 5
Crosby Clo. Felt —7D 6
Cross Deep. Twic —6A 8
Cross Deep Gdns. Twic
—6A 8
Cross Lances Rd. Houn
—1G 7
Cross Rd. SW19 —4K 17
Cross Rd. Felt —1D 12
Cross Rd. King T —4G 15
Cross St. SW13 —6B 4
Cross St. Hamp —2H 13
Crossway. SW20 —1F 23
Crossway. W on T —6A 18
Crossways, The. Surb —5J 21
Crown Arc. King T —6E 14
Crown Clo. W on T —4B 18
Crown La. Mord —1K 23
Crown M. W6 —1D 4
Crown Pas. King T —6E 14
Crown Rd. Mord —1K 23
Crown Rd. N Mald —5K 15
Crown Rd. Twic —3C 8
Crown Ter. Rich —1G 9
Crowntree Clo. Iswth —3A 2
Crowther Av. Bren —1F 3
Crowthorne Clo. SW18
—4J 11
Croxall Ho. W on T —3B 18
Croylands Dri. Surb —4F 21
Crutchfield La. W on T
—6A 18
Cudas Clo. Eps —7C 22
Cuddington Av. Wor Pk
—7C 22
Culsac Rd. Surb —6F 21
Culverhay. Asht —5F 27
Cumberland Clo. SW20
—4G 17
Cumberland Clo. Twic —3C 8
Cumberland Cres. W14
—1H 5

Cumberland Dri. Chess
—7G 21
Cumberland Dri. Esh —6B 20
Cumberland Ho. King T
—4J 15
Cumberland Pl. Sun —1A 18
Cumberland Rd. SW13
—5C 4
Cumberland Rd. Rich —4H 3
Cumbrae Gdns. Surb —6E 20
Cunliffe Rd. Eps —7C 22
Cunnington St. W4 —1K 3
Curlew Ct. Surb —7H 21
Currie Hill Clo. SW19 —1J 17
Curtis Rd. Eps —1K 25
Curtis Rd. Houn —4E 6
Cusack Clo. Twic —1A 14
Cutthroat All. Rich —6D 8
Cyclamen Clo. Hamp —3F 13
Cyclamen Way. Eps —2K 25
Cygnet Av. Felt —4B 6
Cygnets, The. Felt —1D 12
Cypress Av. Twic —4H 7

D'Abernon Clo. Esh —7F 19
Daffodil Pl. Hamp —3F 13
Dagmar Rd. King T —5G 15
Dairy Wlk. SW19 —1H 17
Daisy La. SW6 —7K 5
Daleside Rd. Eps —3K 25
Dale St. W4 —2B 4
Dalewood Gdns. Wor Pk
—6E 22
Dalling Rd. W6 —1E 4
Dalmeny Cres. Houn —1J 7
Dalmeny Rd. Wor Pk —7E 22
Dalmore Av. Clay —3A 24
Damascene Wlk. SE21
—5D 10
Dancer Rd. SW6 —5J 5
Dancer Rd. Rich —7H 3
Danebury Av. SW15 —3B 10
(in two parts)
Danehurst St. SW6 —5H 5
Danemere St. SW15 —7F 5
Danesbury Rd. Felt —5A 6
Danetree Clo. Eps —4K 25
Danetree Rd. Eps —4K 25
Darby Cres. Sun —6B 12
Darby Gdns. Sun —6B 12
D'Arcy Pl. Asht —6G 27
D'Arcy Rd. Asht —6G 27
D'Arcy Rd. Sutt —7G 23
Darell Rd. Rich —7H 3
Darfur St. SW15 —7G 5
Darlan Rd. SW6 —4J 5
Darlaston Rd. SW19 —4G 17
Darley Dri. N Mald —6A 16
Dartmouth Pl. W4 —3B 4
Darwin Rd. W5 —2D 2
Davenport Clo. Tedd —3B 14
Davis Rd. Chess —1H 25
Davmor Ct. Bren —2D 2
Dawes Av. Iswth —2B 8
Dawes Rd. SW6 —4H 5
Dawson Rd. King T —7G 15
Daylesford Av. SW15 —1D 10
Deacon Rd. King T —5G 15
Deacons Ct. Twic —6A 8
Deacons Wlk. Hamp —1F 13
Dealtry Rd. SW15 —1F 11
Deanhill Ct. SW14 —1J 9
Deanhill Rd. SW14 —1J 9
Dean Rd. Hamp —2F 13
Dean Rd. Houn —2G 7
Deans Clo. W4 —3J 3
Deans La. W4 —3J 3
(off Deans Clo.)
Deans Rd. Sutt —7K 23
Deepdale. SW19 —1G 17
Deepwell Clo. Iswth —1B 2
Deerhurst Clo. Felt —1A 14
Dee Rd. Rich —1G 9
Deer Pk. Clo. King T —4J 15
Defoe Av. Rich —4H 3

Delaford St. SW6 —4H 5
Delamere Rd. SW20 —5G 17
Delcombe Av. Wor Pk
—5F 23
Dellbow Rd. Felt —2A 6
Dell, The. Bren —3D 2
Dell, The. Felt —4A 6
Dell Wlk. N Mald —6B 16
Delorme St. W6 —3G 5
Delta Clo. Wor Pk —7C 22
Delta Rd. Wor Pk —7B 22
Delvino Rd. SW6 —5K 5
Dempster Clo. Surb —5D 20
Denbigh Gdns. Rich —2G 9
Dene Clo. Wor Pk —6C 22
Dene Gdns. Th Dit —6B 20
Denehurst Gdns. Rich —1H 9
Denehurst Gdns. Twic —4J 7
Dene Rd. Asht —7G 27
Dene, The. W Mol —2E 18
Denham Rd. Felt —4B 6
Denleigh Gdns. Th Dit
—3K 19
Denman Dri. Clay —2B 24
Denmark Av. SW19 —4H 17
Denmark Ct. Mord —3K 23
Denmark Rd. SW19 —3G 17
Denmark Rd. King T —7F 15
Denmark Rd. Twic —7J 7
Dennan Rd. Surb —5G 21
Denning Clo. Hamp —2E 12
Denningtons, The. Wor Pk
—6B 22
Dennison Gro. SW14 —7A 4
Dennis Pk. Cres. SW20
—5H 17
Dennis Rd. E Mol —1H 19
Denton Gro. W on T —6D 18
Denton Rd. Twic —3E 8
Deodar Rd. SW15 —1H 11
Derby Est. Houn —1G 7
Derby Rd. SW14 —1J 9
Derby Rd. SW19 —4K 17
Derby Rd. Houn —1G 7
Derby Rd. Surb —5H 21
Derek Av. Eps —3H 25
Derek Clo. Ewe —2J 25
Derwent Av. SW15 —1B 16
Derwent Clo. Clay —3A 24
Derwent Lodge. Wor Pk
—6E 22
Derwent Rd. SW20 —2G 23
Derwent Rd. Twic —3G 7
Derwent Yd. W5 —1D 2
(off Derwent Rd.)
Desborough Ho. W14 —3J 5
(off N. End Rd.)
Devas Rd. SW20 —5F 17
Devitt Clo. Asht —5H 27
Devoke Way. W on T —6C 18
Devon Av. Twic —5H 7
Devon Ct. Hamp —4F 13
Devoncroft Gdns. Twic
—4B 8
Devonhurst Pl. W4 —2A 4
Devonshire Dri. Surb —5E 20
Devonshire Gdns. W4 —4K 3
Devonshire M. W4 —2B 4
Devonshire Pas. W4 —2B 4
Devonshire Pl. W4 —2B 4
Devonshire Rd. W4 —2B 4
Devonshire Rd. Felt —7D 6
Devonshire St. W4 —2B 4
Devon Way. Chess —2D 24
Devon Way. Eps —2J 25
Dewsbury Ct. W4 —1K 3
Dewsbury Gdns. Wor Pk
—7D 22
Diana Gdns. Surb —6G 21
Diana Ho. SW13 —5C 4
Dibdin Clo. Sutt —7K 23
Dibdin Rd. Sutt —7K 23
Dickens Clo. Rich —6F 9
Dickenson Rd. Felt —4B 6
Dickerage La. N Mald —7K 15
Dickerage Rd. King T —5K 15

Digby Mans. W6 —2E 4
(off Hammersmith Bri. Rd.)
Digdens Rise. Eps —4K 27
Dilton Gdns. SW15 —5D 10
Dimes Pl. W6 —1E 4
Dinton Rd. King T —4G 15
Disbrowe Rd. W6 —3H 5
Disraeli Clo. W4 —1A 4
Disraeli Gdns. SW15 —1J 11
Disraeli Rd. SW15 —1H 11
Distillery La. W6 —2F 5
Distillery Rd. W6 —2F 5
Distillery Wlk. Bren —3F 3
Ditton Clo. Th Dit —4B 20
Ditton Grange Clo. Surb
—5E 20
Ditton Grange Dri. Surb
—5E 20
Ditton Hill. Surb —5D 20
Ditton Hill Rd. Surb —5D 20
Ditton Lawn. Th Dit —5B 20
Ditton Reach. Th Dit —3C 20
Ditton Rd. Surb —6E 20
Divis Way. SW15 —3E 10
Dock Rd. Bren —4E 2
Dolby Rd. SW6 —6J 5
Dolman Rd. W4 —1A 4
Dolphin Clo. Surb —2E 20
Dolphin Sq. W4 —4B 4
Dolphin St. King T —6F 15
Doneraile St. SW6 —6G 5
Donnington Rd. Wor Pk
—6D 22
Donovan Clo. Eps —6K 25
Doone Clo. Tedd —3B 14
Dora Rd. SW19 —2K 17
Dorchester Gro. W4 —2B 4
Dorchester M. N Mald
—1A 22
Dorchester Rd. Wor Pk
—5F 23
Doria Rd. SW6 —6J 5
Dorien Rd. SW20 —6G 17
Dorking Clo. Wor Pk —6G 23
Dorking Rd. Eps —5H 27
Dormay St. SW18 —2K 11
Dorncliffe Rd. SW6 —6H 5
Dorney Way. Houn —2D 6
Dorset Rd. SW19 —5K 17
Dorset Way. Twic —6J 7
Dorville Cres. W6 —1E 4
Douai Gro. Hamp —5H 13
Douglas Av. N Mald —1E 22
Douglas Ho. Surb —5G 21
Douglas Mans. Houn —1G 7
Douglas Rd. Esh —6G 19
Douglas Rd. Houn —1G 7
Douglas Rd. King T —6J 15
Douglas Rd. Surb —6G 21
Douglas Sq. Mord —3K 23
Dounesforth Gdns. SW18
—5K 11
Dovecote Gdns. SW14 —7A 4
Dover Ho. Rd. SW15 —1D 10
Dover Pk. Dri. SW15 —3E 10
Dowdeswell Clo. SW15
—1B 10
Downbury M. SW18 —2K 11
Downes Clo. Twic —3C 8
Downe Ter. Rich —3F 9
Downfield. Wor Pk —5C 22
Down Hall Rd. King T —5E 14
Down Pl. W6 —1E 4
Down Rd. Tedd —3C 14
Downside. Twic —7A 8
Downs, The. SW20 —4G 17
Down St. W Mol —2F 19
Downs View. Iswth —5A 2
Drake Rd. Chess —2H 25
Drax Av. SW20 —4D 16
Draxmont App. SW19 —3H 17
Draycot Rd. Surb —5H 21
Dray Ct. Wor Pk —6D 22
Drayton Clo. Houn —2E 6
Drive Mans. SW6 —6H 5
(off Fulham Rd.)

Drive, The. SW20 —4F 17
Drive, The. Esh —5H 19
Drive, The. Felt —4B 6
Drive, The. King T —4K 15
Drive, The. Surb —4F 21
Dromore Rd. SW15 —3H 11
Drumaline Ridge. Wor Pk
—6B 22
Drummond Gdns. Eps
—7K 25
Drummond Pl. Twic —3C 8
Dryad St. SW15 —7G 5
Dryburgh Rd. SW15 —7E 4
Ducks Wlk. Twic —2D 8
Dudley Dri. Mord —5H 23
Dudley Gro. Eps —3K 27
Dudley Rd. SW19 —3K 17
Dudley Rd. King T —7G 15
Dudley Rd. Rich —6G 3
Dudley Rd. W on T —4A 18
Duke of Cambridge Clo. Twic
—3J 7
Dukes Av. W4 —2A 4
Duke's Av. W4 —2A 4
Dukes Av. Houn —1D 6
Dukes Av. N Mald —7C 16
Dukes Av. Rich & King T
—1D 14
Dukes Clo. Hamp —2E 12
Dukes Grn. Av. Felt —2A 6
Dukes Head Pas. Hamp
—4H 13
Duke St. Rich —1E 8
Dumbleton Clo. King T
—5J 15
Dunbar Ct. W on T —5B 18
Dunbar Rd. N Mald —1K 21
Duncan Rd. Rich —1F 9
Dundas Gdns. W Mol
—7G 13
Dundonald Rd. SW19
—4H 17
Dungarvan Av. SW15 —1D 10
Dunleary Clo. Houn —4E 6
Dunmore Rd. SW20 —5F 17
Dunmow Rd. Felt —7D 6
Dunsany Rd. W14 —1G 5
Dunsmore Rd. W on T
—3A 18
Dunstable Rd. Rich —1F 9
Dunstable Rd. W Mol —1E 18
Dunstall Rd. SW20 —3E 16
Dunstall Way. W Mol —7G 13
Dunster Av. Mord —5G 23
Dunton Clo. Surb —5F 21
Dunvegan Clo. W Mol
—1G 19
Dupont Rd. SW20 —6G 17
Durban Rd. Chess —1F 25
Durford Cres. SW15 —5E 10
Durham Clo. SW20 —6E 16
Durham Ct. Tedd —1J 13
Durham Rd. SW20 —5E 16
Durham Rd. W5 —1E 2
Durham Rd. Felt —4B 6
Durham Wharf. Bren —4D 2
Durlston Rd. King T —3F 15
Durnsford Av. SW19 —6K 11
Durnsford Rd. SW19 —6K 11
Durrell Rd. SW6 —6J 5
Durrington Av. SW20 —4F 17
Durrington Pk. Rd. SW20
—5F 17
Dutch Gdns. King T —3J 15
Dutch Yd. SW18 —2K 11
Dyer Ho. Hamp —5G 13
Dyers La. SW15 —1E 10
Dymes Path. SW19 —6G 11
Dymock St. SW6 —7K 5
Dynevor Rd. Rich —2F 9
Dysart Av. King T —2D 14

# E

Ealing Pk. Gdns. W5 —1D 2
Ealing Rd. W5 —1E 2
Ealing Rd. Bren —1E 2

Eardley Cres. SW5 —2K 5
Earldom Rd. SW15 —1F 11
Earle Gdns. King T —4F 15
Earl Rd. SW14 —1K 9
Earls Ct. Gdns. SW5 —1K 5
Earls Ct. Sq. SW5 —2K 5
Earls Ter. W8 —1J 5
Earls Wlk. W8 —1K 5
Earne Rd. W4 —3H 3
Earsby St. W14 —1H 5
Eastbank Rd. Hamp —2H 13
Eastbourne Gdns. SW14
—7K 3
Eastbourne Rd. W4 —3K 3
Eastbourne Rd. Bren —2D 2
Eastbourne Rd. Felt —6C 6
Eastbury Gro. W4 —2B 4
Eastbury Rd. King T —4F 15
Eastcote Av. W Mol —2E 18
Eastdean Av. Eps —2J 27
East La. King T —7E 14
Eastleigh Wlk. SW15 —4D 10
Eastmont Rd. Esh —6A 20
East Rd. King T —5F 15
E. Sheen Av. SW14 —2A 10
East St. Bren —4D 2
Eastway. Eps —7K 25
Eastway. Mord —2G 23
Eaton Dri. King T —4H 15
Eaton Rd. Houn —1J 7
Ebbas Way. Eps —4J 27
Ebbisham Rd. Eps —3J 27
Ebbisham Rd. Wor Pk
—6F 23
Ebor Cotts. SW15 —7B 10
Eddiscombe Rd. SW6 —6J 5
Ede Clo. Houn —1E 6
Edenfield Gdns. Wor Pk
—7C 22
Edenhurst Av. SW6 —7J 5
Edensor Gdns. W4 —4B 4
Edensor Rd. W4 —4B 4
Eden St. King T —6E 14
Eden Wlk. King T —6F 15
Edgar Ct. N Mald —7B 16
Edgarley Ter. SW6 —5H 5
Edgar Rd. Houn —4E 6
Edgecoombe Clo. King T
—4A 16
Edge Hill. SW19 —4G 17
Edge Hill Ct. SW19 —4G 17
Edgehill Ct. W on T —5B 18
Edinburgh Ct. SW20 —2G 23
Edith Gdns. Surb —4J 21
Edith Ho. W6 —2F 5
(off Queen Caroline St.)
Edith Rd. W14 —1H 5
Edith Vs. W14 —1J 5
Edna Rd. SW20 —6G 17
Edward Clo. Hamp —2H 13
Edwardes Pl. W8 —1J 5
Edwardes Sq. W8 —1J 5
Edward Rd. Hamp —2H 13
Edwards Clo. Wor Pk
—6G 23
Edwin Rd. Twic —5K 7
Edwinstray Ho. Felt —7F 7
Eel Pie Island. Twic —5B 8
Effie Pl. SW6 —4K 5
Effie Rd. SW6 —4K 5
Effingham Rd. Surb —4C 20
Effra Rd. SW19 —3K 17
Egerton Rd. N Mald —1C 22
Egerton Rd. Twic —4K 7
Egham Clo. SW19 —6H 11
Egham Clo. Sutt —6H 23
Egham Cres. Sutt —7G 23
Egleston Rd. Mord —3K 23
Egliston M. SW15 —7F 5
Egliston Rd. SW15 —7F 5
Egmont Av. Surb —5G 21
Egmont Rd. N Mald —1C 22
Egmont Rd. Surb —5G 21
Egmont Rd. Sutt —7A 24
Egmont Rd. W on T —4A 18
Elborough St. SW18 —5K 11
Eleanor Av. Eps —6K 25

Eleanor Gro. SW13 —7F
Electric Pde. Surb —3E
Elfin Gro. Tedd —2A 14
Elgar Av. Surb —5H 21
Elizabeth Cotts. Rich —
Elizabeth Ct. Tedd —2K
Elizabeth Gdns. Sun —
Elizabeth Way. Felt —1E
Elladine Rd. W6 —3G 5
Elland Rd. W on T —6C
Ellenborough Pl. SW15
Elleray Rd. Tedd —3A 1
Ellerby St. SW6 —5G 5
Ellerdine Rd. Houn —1H
Ellerker Gdns. Rich —3F
Ellerman Av. Twic —5B
Ellerton Rd. SW13 —5C
Ellerton Rd. SW20 —4D
Ellerton Rd. Surb —6G
Ellesmere Ct. W4 —3A
Ellesmere Rd. W4 —3K
Ellesmere Rd. Twic —3
Elleswood Ct. Surb —4
Ellingham Rd. Chess —
Elliot Gdns. SW15 —1D
Elliott Rd. W4 —1B 4
Ellisfield Dri. SW15 —4
Ellison Rd. SW13 —6C
Elm Bank Gdns. SW13 –
Elmbridge Av. Surb —2
Elm Clo. SW20 —1F 23
Elm Clo. Surb —4K 21
Elm Clo. Twic —6G 7
Elm Ct. W Mol —1G 19
Elm Cres. King T —5F 1
Elmcroft Clo. Chess —7
Elmcroft Dri. Chess —7
Elmdene. Surb —5K 21
Elm Dri. Sun —6B 12
Elmer Gdns. Iswth —1J
Elmers Dri. Tedd —3C 1
Elmfield Av. Tedd —2A
Elm Gdns. Clay —3A 24
Elmgate Av. Felt —7B 6
Elm Gro. SW19 —4H 1
Elm Gro. Eps —3K 27
Elm Gro. King T —5F 1
Elm Gro. Rd. SW13 —5
Elm Lodge. SW6 —5G
Elm Rd. SW14 —7K 3
Elm Rd. Chess —1F 25
Elm Rd. Clay —3A 24
Elm Rd. King T —5G 15
Elm Rd. N Mald —6A 1
Elm Rd. W. Sutt —4J 2
Elmshaw Rd. SW15 —2
Elmsleigh Ho. Twic —6
(off Staines Rd.)
Elmsleigh Rd. Twic —6
Elmslie Clo. Eps —3K 2
Elmstead Gdns. Wor Pk
Elms, The. SW13 —7C
Elmstone Rd. SW6 —5
Elm Tree Av. Esh —4J 1
Elmtree Rd. Tedd —5A
Elm Wlk. SW20 —1F 23
Elm Way. Wor Pk —7F
Elmwood Av. Felt —6A
Elmwood Clo. Asht —6
Elmwood Rd. W4 —3K
Elsenham St. SW18 —5
Elsinore Way. Rich —7J
Elsrick Av. Mord —2K 2
Elstead Ct. Sutt —5H 2
Elsworthy. Th Dit —3K
Elthiron Rd. SW6 —5K
Elthorne Ct. Felt —5B 6
Elton Clo. King T —4D
Elton Rd. King T —6F 1
Ely Clo. SW20 —6C 16
Elysium Pl. SW6 —6J 5
(off Elysium St.)
Elysium St. SW6 —6J 5

nkment. SW15 —6G **5**
nkment, The. Twic
—5B **8**
Ct. Rd. Th Dit —3K **19**
Farm Av. E Mol
—3J **19**
Farm Way. E Mol
Gdns. Th Dit —4K **19**
La. Esh & E Mol
—4J **19**
ton Wlk. Hamp —2E **12**
Rd. W12 —1C **4**
Pl. King T —6E **14**
ess Pl. SW6 —2K **5**
vour Way. SW19
—1K **17**
eigh Gdns. Surb
—3D **20**

Vay. Surb —4H **21**
Rd. Bren —2E **2**
Wlk. Bren —2E **2**
line St. SW6 —2K **5**
re Gdns. SW14 —2A **10**
re Rd. SW15 —1F **11**
dale Rd. Rich —6G **3**
more Av. W4 —1C **4**
more Gdns. Th Dit
—3K **19**
orise Way. SW18
—1K **11**
orise Way. Tedd
—3A **14**
s M. SW6 —4K **5**
Rd. SW6 —4J **5**
Rd. SW6 —5J **5**
n Gap. Lea —4C **26**
n Rd. Asht —7G **27**
n Rd. Sutt & Mord
—4J **23**
rth Rd. Iswth —4C **2**
on Clo. SW18 —2K **11**
oft Way. Twic —3A **8**
t Gdns. W4 —3J **3**
t Rd. King T —6J **15**
t Sq. King T —6J **15**
Rd. SW20 —4E **16**
aw Pl. SW15 —2H **11**
e Rd. SW19 —6K **17**
Gdns. N Mald —1D **22**
Av. Sutt —7G **23**
Av. W on T —4A **18**
Gdns. SW19 —6G **11**
Grn. Esh —7G **19**
Grn. Dri. Esh —7G **19**
Pl. Av. Esh —7G **19**
Rd. E Mol —3J **19**
nd Gdns. W4 —1A **4**
nd Rd. W4 —1A **4**
nd St. SW15 —1H **11**
Av. Iswth —1K **7**
Clo. Mord —4G **23**
Ct. SW13 —6C **4**
Pl. W4 —1K **3**
Pl. Sq. W4 —1A **4**
Rd. W4 —1A **4**
urt Rd. SW6 —4J **5**
a Av. N Mald —1E **22**
ge Clo. Houn —1F **7**
t Wlk. SW6 —5G **5**
oert Rd. SW20 —5G **17**
Av. N Mald —2A **22**
St. Rich —2F **9**
Pl. Surb —3G **21**
a Rd. King T —6H **15**
ce Rd. SW6 —4K **5**
Ho. Felt —6F **7**
Clo. Twic —4G **7**
Gdns. Rich —1F **9**
Rd. SW19 —2K **17**
Rd. W4 —1A **4**
Rd. Ham —7D **8**
Rd. Rich —7F **3**
Ter. Rich —7F **3**

Evenwood Clo. SW15
Everatt Clo. SW18 —3J **11**
Everdon Rd. SW13 —3D **4**
Everington St. W6 —3G **5**
Eve Rd. Iswth —1B **8**
Eversfield Rd. Rich —6G **3**
Eversley Pk. SW19 —3E **16**
Eversley Rd. Surb —1G **21**
Ewald Rd. SW6 —6J **5**
Ewell Rd. Dit H —4C **20**
Ewell Rd. Surb —3F **21**
Excelsior Clo. King T —6H **15**
*Exeter Ho. Felt —6D 6*
*(off Watermill Way)*
Exeter Rd. Felt —7E **6**
Eyot Gdns. W6 —2C **4**
Eyot Grn. W4 —2C **4**

**F**abian Rd. SW6 —4J **5**
Fagg's Rd. Felt —2A **6**
Fairacre. N Mald —7B **16**
Fairacres. SW15 —1D **10**
Fairburn Ct. SW15 —2H **11**
*Fairburn Ho. W14 —2J 5*
*(off Ivatt Pl.)*
Faircroft Ct. Tedd —3B **14**
Fairdale Gdns. SW15 —1E **10**
Fairfax Clo. W on T —5A **18**
Fairfax Rd. W4 —1B **4**
Fairfax Rd. Tedd —3B **14**
Fairfield Av. Twic —5G **7**
Fairfield E. King T —6F **15**
Fairfield N. King T —6F **15**
Fairfield Pl. King T —7F **15**
Fairfield Rd. King T —6F **15**
Fairfield S. King T —7F **15**
Fairfield W. King T —6F **15**
Fairfields Rd. Houn —1H **7**
Fairford Gdns. Wor Pk
—7C **22**
Fairholme Cres. Asht —6D **26**
Fairholme Rd. W14 —2H **5**
Fairlands Av. Sutt —6K **23**
Fairlawn Av. W4 —1K **3**
Fair Lawn Clo. King T —3A **24**
Fairlawn Clo. King T —3K **15**
Fairlawn Ct. W4 —1K **3**
Fairlawn Ct. Felt —1E **12**
Fairlawn Gro. W4 —1K **3**
Fairlawn Rd. SW19 —4J **17**
Fairlawns. Twic —3D **8**
Fairlight Clo. Wor Pk —7F **23**
Fairmead. Surb —5J **21**
Fairmead Clo. N Mald
—7A **16**
Fairmead Ct. Rich —6J **3**
Fairoak La. Oxs & Chess
—7A **24**
Fairway. SW20 —7F **17**
Fairway Clo. Eps —1K **25**
Fairway Clo. Houn —2B **6**
Fairways. Tedd —4E **14**
Fairway, The. Lea —7B **26**
Fairway, The. N Mald —5A **16**
Fairway, The. W Mol —7G **13**
Falcon Clo. W4 —3K **3**
Falcon Rd. Hamp —4E **12**
Falcon Way. Felt —2A **6**
Falstaff M. Hamp —5H **13**
Fane St. W14 —3J **5**
Fanshawe Rd. Rich —1D **14**
Fanthorpe St. SW15 —7F **5**
Faraday Rd. SW19 —3K **17**
Faraday Rd. W Mol —1F **19**
Fareham Rd. Felt —4B **6**
Farlington Pl. SW15 —4E **10**
Farlow Rd. SW15 —7G **5**
*Farm Clo. SW6 —4K 5*
*(off Farm La.)*
Farm La. SW6 —3K **5**
Farm La. Asht & Eps —6H **27**
Farm Rd. Esh —6G **19**
Farm Rd. Houn —5D **6**
Farm Way. Wor Pk —7F **23**

Farnell M. SW5 —2K **5**
Farnell Rd. Iswth —1J **7**
Farnham Gdns. SW20
—6E **16**
Faroe Rd. W14 —1G **5**
Farquhar Rd. SW19 —7K **11**
Farrer Ct. Twic —4E **8**
Farrier Clo. Sun —7K **13**
Farthings, The. King T
—5H **15**
Fassett Rd. King T —1F **21**
*Fauconberg Ct. W4 —3K 3*
*(off Fauconberg Rd.)*
Fauconberg Rd. W4 —3K **3**
Favart Rd. SW6 —5K **5**
Fawcus Clo. Clay —3A **24**
Fawe Pk. Rd. SW15 —1J **11**
Fearnley Cres. Hamp —2D **12**
Fee Farm Rd. Clay —4A **24**
Felcott Clo. W on T —7B **18**
Felcott Rd. W on T —7B **18**
Felden St. SW6 —5J **5**
Felgate M. W6 —1E **4**
Felix Rd. W on T —3A **18**
Fellbrook. Rich —7F **3**
Felsham Rd. SW15 —7F **5**
Feltham Av. E Mol —1K **19**
Felthambrook Way. Felt
—7A **6**
Felthamhill Rd. Felt —1A **12**
Fendall Rd. Eps —2K **25**
Fenelon Pl. W14 —1J **5**
Fenn Ho. Iswth —5C **2**
Ferguson Av. Surb —2G **21**
Fernbank Av. W on T —4D **18**
Fern Gro. Felt —4A **6**
Fernhill Gdns. King T —2E **14**
Fernhurst Rd. SW6 —5H **5**
Fernside Av. Felt —1A **12**
Ferry La. SW13 —3C **4**
Ferry La. Bren —3F **3**
Ferry La. Rich —3G **3**
Ferrymoor. Rich —7C **8**
Ferry Rd. SW13 —4D **4**
Ferry Rd. Tedd —2C **14**
Ferry Rd. Th Dit —3C **20**
Ferry Rd. Twic —5C **8**
Ferry Rd. W Mol —7F **13**
Ferry Sq. Bren —4F **3**
Festing Rd. SW15 —7G **5**
Field Clo. Chess —2D **24**
Field Clo. W Mol —2G **19**
Fieldcommon La. W on T
—5D **18**
Field Ct. SW19 —7K **11**
Field End. Twic —1A **14**
Fielding Av. Twic —7H **7**
*Fielding Ho. W4 —3B 4*
*(off Devonshire Rd.)*
Field La. Bren —4D **2**
Field La. Tedd —2B **14**
Field Pl. N Mald —3C **22**
Field Rd. W6 —2H **5**
Field Rd. Felt —3A **6**
Fife Rd. SW14 —2K **9**
Fife Rd. King T —6F **15**
Fifth Cross Rd. Twic —6J **7**
Filby Rd. Chess —3G **25**
Filmer Rd. SW6 —5H **5**
Finborough Rd. SW10 —2K **5**
Finch Dri. Felt —4C **6**
Findon Clo. SW18 —3K **11**
Finlays Clo. Chess —2H **25**
Finlay St. SW6 —5G **5**
Fir Clo. W on T —4A **18**
Firdene. Surb —5K **21**
Fire Bell La. Surb —3F **21**
Fir Gro. N Mald —4B **22**
Fir Rd. Felt —2C **12**
Fir Rd. Sutt —5J **23**
Firs Av. SW14 —1K **9**
Firs Clo. Clay —3A **24**
First Av. SW14 —7B **4**
First Av. W on T —3A **18**
First Av. W Mol —1E **18**

First Clo. W Mol —7H **13**
First Cross Rd. Twic —6K **7**
First Slip. Lea —7B **26**
Firstway. SW20 —6F **17**
Firth Gdns. SW6 —5H **5**
Fir Tree Rd. Houn —1D **6**
Fisher Clo. W on T —7A **18**
Fisherman Clo. Rich —1D **14**
Fisherman's Pl. W4 —3C **4**
Fishers Dene. Clay —4B **24**
Fisher's La. W4 —1A **4**
Fitzalan Rd. Clay —4A **24**
Fitzgeorge Av. W14 —1H **5**
Fitzgeorge Av. N Mald
—5A **16**
Fitzgerald Av. SW14 —7B **4**
Fitzgerald Rd. SW14 —7A **4**
Fitzgerald Rd. Th Dit —3B **20**
Fitzjames Av. W14 —1H **5**
Fitzroy Cres. W4 —4A **4**
Fitzwilliam Av. Rich —6G **3**
Fitzwilliam Ho. Rich —1E **8**
Fitzwygram Clo. Hamp
—2H **13**
Flanders Mans. W4 —1C **4**
Flanders Rd. W4 —1B **4**
Flaxley Rd. Mord —4K **23**
*Flaxman Ho. W4 —2B 4*
*(off Devonshire St.)*
Fleece Rd. Surb —5D **20**
Fleet Clo. W Mol —2E **18**
Fleet La. W Mol —3E **18**
Fleetside. W Mol —2E **18**
Fleetwood Clo. Chess —4E **24**
Fleetwood Rd. King T —7J **15**
Fleetwood Sq. King T —7J **15**
Fleming Way. Iswth —1A **8**
Fleur Gates. SW19 —4G **11**
Flood La. Twic —5B **8**
*Flora Gdns. W6 —1E 4*
*(off Albion Gdns.)*
Floral Ct. Asht —7D **26**
Florence Clo. W on T —4A **18**
Florence Gdns. W4 —3K **3**
Florence Rd. SW19 —3K **17**
Florence Rd. Felt —5A **6**
Florence Rd. King T —4G **15**
Florence Rd. W on T —4A **18**
Florence Ter. SW15 —7B **10**
Florian Rd. SW15 —1H **11**
Floss St. SW15 —6F **5**
Foley M. Clay —3A **24**
Foley Rd. Clay —3A **24**
Fontley Way. SW15 —4D **10**
Footpath, The. SW15 —2D **10**
Fordbridge Rd. Sun —1A **18**
Foreman Ct. W6 —1F **5**
Foreman Ct. Twic —5A **8**
Forest Cres. Asht —5H **27**
Forest Rd. Felt —6B **6**
Forest Rd. Rich —4H **3**
Forest Side. Wor Pk —5C **22**
Forest Way. Asht —6H **27**
Forge Dri. Clay —4B **24**
Forge La. Felt —2D **12**
Forge La. Sun —7A **12**
Fortescue Av. Twic —7H **7**
Forty Footpath. SW14 —7K **3**
Forum, The. W Mol —1G **19**
Foskett Rd. SW6 —6J **5**
Foster Rd. W4 —2A **4**
Fountains Av. Felt —7E **6**
Fountains Clo. Felt —6E **6**
Four Seasons Cres. Sutt
—6J **23**
Four Sq. Ct. Houn —3F **7**
Fourth Cross Rd. Twic —6J **7**
Foxcombe Rd. SW15 —5D **10**
Foxglove La. Chess —1H **25**
Foxwarren. Clay —5A **24**
Foxwood Clo. Felt —7A **6**
Francis Clo. Eps —7A **22**
Francis Gro. SW19 —6H **11**
Franklin Clo. King T —7H **15**
Franklin Sq. W14 —2J **5**

Franklyn Rd. W on T —3A **18**
Franks Av. N Mald —1K **21**
Fraser Ho. Bren —2G **3**
Fraser St. W4 —2B **4**
Freehold Ind. Cen. Houn
—2B **6**
Freeman Dri. W Mol —7E **12**
French St. Sun —6B **12**
Frensham Dri. SW15 —7C **10**
Freshmount Gdns. Eps
—7J **25**
Friars Av. SW15 —7C **10**
Friars La. Rich —2E **8**
Friars Stile Pl. Rich —3F **9**
Friars Stile Rd. Rich —3F **9**
Frimley Clo. SW19 —6H **11**
Frimley Rd. Chess —2E **24**
Friston St. SW6 —6K **5**
Fritham Clo. N Mald —3B **22**
Frogmore. SW18 —2K **11**
Frogmore Clo. Sutt —7H **23**
Frogmore Gdns. Sutt —7H **23**
Fulham B'way. SW6 —4K **5**
Fulham High St. SW6 —6H **5**
Fulham Pal. Rd. W6 & SW6
—2F **5**
Fulham Pk. Gdns. SW6 —6J **5**
Fulham Pk. Rd. SW6 —6J **5**
Fulham Rd. SW6 —6H **5**
Fullbrooks Av. Wor Pk
—5C **22**
Fullers Av. Surb —6G **21**
Fullers Way N. Surb —7G **21**
Fullers Way S. Chess —1F **25**
Fulmar Ct. Surb —3G **21**
Fulmer Clo. Hamp —2D **12**
Fulmer Way. W13 —1C **2**
Fulstone Clo. Houn —1E **6**
Fulwell Pk. Av. Twic —6G **7**
Fulwell Rd. Tedd —1J **13**
Fulwood Gdns. Twic —3A **8**
Fulwood Wlk. SW19 —5H **11**
Furber St. W6 —1E **4**
Furrows, The. W on T
—6B **18**

**G**abriel Clo. Felt —1D **12**
Gadesden Rd. Eps —3K **25**
(in two parts)
Gainsborough Clo. Esh
—5K **19**
*Gainsborough Ct. W4 —2J 3*
*(off Chaseley Dri.)*
Gainsborough Gdns. Iswth
—2J **7**
Gainsborough Rd. W4 —1C **4**
Gainsborough Rd. Eps
—6K **25**
Gainsborough Rd. N Mald
—4A **22**
Gainsborough Rd. Rich
—6G **3**
Galata Rd. SW13 —4D **4**
Galba Ct. Bren —4E **2**
Gale Clo. Hamp —3D **12**
Galena Rd. W6 —1E **4**
Galgate Clo. SW19 —5H **11**
Galsworthy Rd. King T
—5J **15**
Galveston Rd. SW15 —2J **11**
Gamlen Rd. SW15 —1G **11**
Gander Grn. La. Sutt —6H **23**
Gap Rd. SW19 —2K **17**
Garden Clo. SW15 —4F **11**
Garden Clo. Hamp —2E **12**
Garden Ct. W4 —1K **3**
Garden Ct. Hamp —2E **12**
Garden Rd. Rich —7H **3**
Gardener Gro. Felt —6E **6**
Gardens, The. Esh —7F **19**
Gardner Ho. Felt —6E **6**
Garendon Gdns. Mord
—4K **23**

ton Clo. Eps —1K 27
ton Cres. Houn —2G 7
ton Ho. W4 —3B 4
ton Pl. Sun —4A 12
ton Rd. Bren —3E 2
ton Rd. Twic —5K 7
et Ct. W6 —1D 4
et Gdns. W6 —1D 4
hersmith Bri. SW13 &
    W6 —3E 4
hersmith Bri. Rd. W6
wo parts) —2E 4
hersmith B'way. W6
    —1F 5
hersmith Flyover. W6
    —2F 5
hersmith Gro. W6 —3F 5
hersmith Ind. Est. W6
    —3F 5
hersmith Rd. W6 & W14
    —1G 5
hersmith Ter. W6
    —2D 4
hond Clo. Hamp —5F 13
den Rd. King T —7H 15
shire Hog La. W6
    —1E 4
ton Clo. SW20 —4F 17
ton Ct. Av. E Mol
    —2J 19
ton Ct. Bri. E Mol
    —1K 19
ton Ct. Pde. E Mol
    —1K 19
ton Ct. Rd. E Mol &
    King T —6J 13
ton Ct. Rd. Hamp
    —6H 13
ton Ct. Way. Th Dit &
    E Mol —6K 19
ton Farm Ind. Est. Felt
    —7D 6
ton La. Felt —1D 6
ton Rd. Hamp & Tedd
    —2J 13
ton Rd. Twic —7J 7
ton Rd. Wor Pk —6E 22
ton Rd. E. Felt —1E 12
ton Rd. W. Felt —7D 6
Ridings. Rich —2G 15
Sq. Rich —6D 8
St. Rich —5C 8
The. Bren —4D 2
n Ct. SW19 —4G 17
side Clo. Wor Pk
    —5G 23
ard Clo. SW18 —5K 11
ord Row. SW19 —3F 17
ell Rd. SW6 —4H 5
ver Clo. Rich —4H 3
ver Clo. Sutt —7H 23
ver Ct. SW15 —1C 10
ver Ter. Iswth —5B 2
ier Gro. E Mol —1J 19
on Clo. SW14 —7K 3
orth Rd. Felt —5A 6
orth Rd. Hamp —1E 12
orth Rd. Houn —5D 6
orth Rd. Sun —4A 12
orth Ter. Houn —1G 7
orth Trading Est. Felt
    —7D 6
edown Rd. SW6 —5K 5
ord St. SW6 —5G 5
idge Av. SW15 —4C 10
urt Clo. Iswth —7B 2
urt Rd. SW19 —4K 17
wicke Rd. W4 —1A 4
wicke Rd. Rich —1D 14
wicks Way. SW18
    —2K 11
ys Clo. E Mol —1K 19
ield. Esh —7K 19
La. Clay —3A 24
wood Rd. Iswth —4A 2

Harfield Rd. Sun —6C 12
Harlequin Av. Bren —3B 2
Harlequin Clo. Iswth —2K 7
Harlequin Rd. Tedd —4C 14
Harlington Rd. E. Felt —4A 6
Harlington Rd. W. Felt —3A 6
Harriott's La. Asht —7D 26
Harrow Clo. Chess —4E 24
Harrowdene Gdns. Tedd
    —4B 14
Harrow Pas. King T —6E 14
Hartfield Cres. SW19 —4J 17
Hartfield Rd. SW19 —4J 17
Hartfield Rd. Chess —2E 24
Hartford Rd. Eps —3J 25
Hartham Clo. Iswth —5B 2
Hartham Rd. Iswth —5A 2
Hartington Ct. W4 —4J 3
Hartington Rd. W4 —4J 3
Hartington Rd. Twic —4C 8
Hartismere Rd. SW6 —4J 5
Hartland Rd. Hamp —1G 13
Hartland Rd. Iswth —7B 2
Hartland Rd. Mord —4K 23
Hartland Way. Mord —4J 23
Hartop Point. SW6 —4H 5
    (off Pellant Rd.)
Harvard Hill. W4 —3J 3
Harvard La. W4 —2K 3
Harvard Rd. W4 —2J 3
Harvester Rd. Eps —6K 25
Harvesters Clo. Iswth —2J 7
Harvest La. Th Dit —3B 20
Harvey Ho. Bren —2F 3
Harvey Rd. Houn —4E 6
Harwood Rd. SW6 —4K 5
Haslam Av. Sutt —5H 23
Haslemere Av. W7 & W13
    —1B 2
Haslemere Av. Houn —6A 8
Haslemere Clo. Hamp —2E 12
Hastings Ct. Tedd —2J 13
Hatch Pl. King T —2G 15
Hatfield Mead. Mord —2K 23
Hatfield Rd. Asht —7G 27
Hatfield Rd. Chess
    —2E 24
Hatherleigh Clo. Mord
    —1K 23
Hatherley Rd. Rich —6G 3
Hatherop Rd. Hamp —4E 12
Havana Rd. SW19 —6K 11
Haven Clo. SW19 —7G 11
Haven, The. Rich —7H 3
Haverfield Gdns. Rich —4H 3
Haversham Clo. Twic —3E 8
Hawkesbury Rd. SW15
    —2E 10
Hawkesley Clo. Twic —1B 14
Hawkewood Rd. Sun —7A 12
Hawkfield Ct. Iswth —6A 2
Hawkhurst Gdns. Chess
    —1F 25
Hawkhurst Way. N Mald
    —2A 22
Hawkins Rd. Tedd —3C 14
Hawksmoor St. W6 —3G 5
Hawks Rd. King T —6G 15
Hawley Clo. Hamp —3E 12
Hawthorn Av. Rich —6F 3
Hawthorn Clo. Hamp —2F 13
Hawthorn Gdns. W5 —1E 2
Hawthorn Hatch. Bren —4C 2
Haycroft Rd. Surb —6E 20
Haydon Pk. Rd. SW19
    —2K 17
Hayes Cres. Sutt —7G 23
Haygarth Pl. SW19 —2G 17
Haygreen Clo. King T —3J 15
Haylett Gdns. King T —1E 20
Hayling Ct. Sutt —7F 23
Haymer Gdns. Wor Pk
    —7D 22
Haynt Wlk. SW20 —7H 17
Hayward Gdns. SW15
    —3F 11

Hazel Bank. Surb —5K 21
Hazelbury Clo. SW19 —6K 17
Hazel Clo. Bren —4C 2
Hazel Clo. Twic —4H 7
Hazel La. Rich —6F 9
Hazelwood Ct. Surb —3F 21
Hazledene Rd. W4 —3K 3
Hazlemere Gdns. Wor Pk
    —5D 22
Hazlewell Rd. SW15 —2F 11
Hazlitt Clo. Felt —1D 12
Hazlitt M. W14 —1H 5
Hazlitt Rd. W14 —1H 5
Hazon Way. Eps —1K 27
Headley Clo. Eps —3H 25
Headley Rd. Eps —7J 27
Headway Clo. Rich —1D 14
Hearne Rd. W4 —3H 3
Heatham Pk. Twic —4A 8
Heath Bus. Cen. Houn —1H 7
Heathcote Rd. Twic —3C 8
Heath Ct. Houn —1E 6
Heathdale Av. Houn —1D 6
Heath Dri. SW20 —1F 23
Heather Clo. Hamp —5E 12
Heather Clo. Iswth —2J 7
Heatherdale Clo. King T
    —4H 15
Heather Wlk. Twic —4F 7
    (off Stephenson Rd.)
Heathfield Ct. W4 —2A 4
Heathfield Gdns. W4 —2K 3
Heathfield N. Twic —4K 7
Heathfields Ct. Houn —2D 6
Heathfield S. Twic —4K 7
Heathfield Ter. W4 —2K 3
Heath Gdns. Twic —5A 8
Heathlands Clo. Twic —6A 8
Heathlands Way. Houn —2D 6
Heathmans Rd. SW6 —5J 5
Heath Mead. SW19 —7G 11
Heath Rise. SW15 —3G 11
Heath Rd. Houn —5A 8
Heath Rd. Twic —5A 8
Heathrow International Trading
    Est. Houn —1A 6
Heathside. Esh —7K 19
Heathside. Houn —4E 6
Heathside Clo. Esh —7K 19
Heathview Gdns. SW15
    —4F 11
Hebron Rd. W6 —1F 5
Heckfield Pl. SW6 —4K 5
Heddon Clo. Iswth —1B 8
Hedley Rd. Twic —4F 7
Heights Clo. SW20 —4E 16
Heldmann Clo. Houn —1J 7
Helen Av. Felt —4A 6
Helen Clo. W Mol —1G 19
Helme Clo. SW19 —2J 17
Hemming Clo. Hamp —5F 13
Hemmingford Rd. Sutt
    —7G 23
Hemsby Rd. Chess —3G 24
Henfield Rd. SW19 —5J 17
Henley Av. Sutt —7H 23
Henley Clo. Iswth —5A 2
Henley Dri. King T —4C 16
Henley Way. Felt —2C 12
Henrietta Ho. W6 —2F 5
    (off Queen Caroline St.)
Henry Jackson Rd. SW15
    —7G 5
Henty Wlk. SW15 —2E 10
Hepple Clo. Iswth —6C 2
Hepplestone Clo. SW15
    —3E 10
Herbert Gdns. W4 —3J 3
Herbert Morrison Ho. SW6
    (off Clem Attlee Ct.) —3J 5
Herbert Rd. SW19 —4J 17
    (in two parts)
Herbert Rd. King T —7G 15
Hereford Gdns. Twic —5H 7
Hereford Rd. W5 —1D 2
Hereford Rd. Felt —5B 6

Hereford Way. Chess —2D 24
Hermitage Clo. Clay —3B 24
Hermitage, The. SW13 —5C 4
Hermitage, The. Rich —2F 9
Herne Rd. Surb —6E 20
Heron Rd. Twic —1B 8
Heron's Pl. Iswth —7C 2
Heron Sq. Rich —2E 8
Hersham Clo. SW15 —4D 10
Hersham Gdns. W on T
    —7B 18
Hersham Rd. W on T —5A 18
Hersham Trading Est. W on T
    —6D 18
Hertford Av. SW14 —2A 10
Hestercombe Av. SW6 —6H 5
Hexham Gdns. Iswth —4B 2
Hexham Rd. Mord —5K 23
Heyford Av. SW20 —7J 17
Heythorp St. SW18 —5J 11
Hibernia Gdns. Houn —1F 7
Hibernia Rd. Houn —1F 7
Hickey's Almshouses. Rich
    —1G 9
Hidcote Gdns. SW20 —7E 16
Highbury Clo. N Mald
    —1K 21
Highbury Rd. SW19 —2H 17
High Cedar Dri. SW20
    —4F 17
Highclere Rd. N Mald —7A 16
Highcliffe Dri. SW15 —3C 10
High Coombe Pl. King T
    —4A 16
Highcross Way. SW15
    —5D 10
Highdown. Wor Pk —2E 22
Highdown Rd. SW15 —3E 10
High Dri. N Mald —5K 15
Highfield. Felt —5A 6
Highfield Clo. Surb —5D 20
Highfield Rd. Felt —6A 6
Highfield Rd. Iswth —5A 2
Highfield Rd. Surb —4K 21
Highfield Rd. W on T —5B 18
Highfields. Asht —7E 26
Highfields. Sutt —6K 23
High Foleys. Clay —4C 24
Highlands Heath. SW15
    —4F 11
High Pk. Av. Rich —5H 3
High Pk. Rd. Rich —5H 3
High St. Brentford, Bren
    —4D 2
High St. Claygate, Clay
    —3A 24
High St. East Molesey, E Mol
    —1F 19
High St. Epsom, Eps —2K 27
High St. Esher, Esh —7H 19
High St. Feltham, Felt —6A 6
High St. Hampton, Hamp
    —5H 13
High St. Hampton Wick,
    Hamp W —5D 14
High St. Hampton Hill, Hamp H
    —3H 13
High St. Hounslow, Houn
    —1G 7
High St. Kingston upon
    Thames, King T —7E 14
High St. M. SW19 —2H 17
High St. New Malden, N Mald
    —1B 22
High St. Teddington, Tedd
    —3D 14
High St. Thames Ditton, Th Dit
    —3B 20
High St. Whitton, Twic
    —4H 7
High St. Wimbledon, SW19
    —2G 17
Hilary Clo. SW6 —7K 5
Hilbert Rd. Sutt —7G 23
Hilda Ct. Surb —4E 20
Hilders, The. Asht —6J 27

Hildyard Rd. SW6 —3K 5
Hillary Cres. W on T —5B 18
Hillbrow. N Mald —7C 16
Hillbrow Rd. Esh —7H 19
Hill Cres. Surb —2G 21
Hill Cres. Wor Pk —6F 23
Hillcrest Gdns. Esh —7A 20
Hillcross Av. Mord —3G 23
Hillersdon Av. SW13 —6D 4
Hill Field Rd. Hamp —4E 12
Hillier Lodge. Tedd —2J 13
Hillmont Rd. Esh —7K 19
Hill Rise. Esh —6C 20
Hill Rise. Rich —2E 8
Hillside. SW19 —3G 17
Hillside Clo. Mord —1H 23
Hillside Rd. Asht —6G 27
Hillside Rd. Surb —1H 21
Hill St. Rich —2E 8
Hill Top. Mord —3K 23
Hill Top. Sutt —4J 23
Hillview. SW20 —4E 16
Hill View Rd. Clay —4B 24
Hill View Rd. Twic —3B 8
Hinchley Clo. Esh —1A 24
Hinchley Dri. Esh —7A 20
Hinchley Way. Esh —7B 20
Hinton Av. Houn —1C 6
Hobart Pl. Rich —4G 9
Hobart Rd. Wor Pk —7E 22
Hobbes Wlk. SW15 —2E 10
Hobill Wlk. Surb —5G 21
Hogarth La. W4 —3B 4
Hogarth Pl. SW5 —1K 5
    (off Hogarth Rd.)
Hogarth Rd. SW5 —1K 5
Hogarth Ter. W4 —3B 4
Hogarth Way. Hamp —5H 13
Hogsmill Way. Eps —2K 25
Holbrooke Pl. Rich —2E 8
Holcombe St. W6 —1E 4
Holland Av. SW20 —5C 16
Holland Rd. W14 —1J 5
Hollands, The. Felt —1C 12
Hollands, The. Wor Pk
    —5C 22
Holles Clo. Hamp —3F 13
Hollies Clo. Twic —6A 8
Hollies Rd. W5 —1D 2
Hollingsworth Ct. Surb
    —4E 20
Hollington Cres. N Mald
    —3C 22
Hollows, The. Bren —3G 3
Holly Av. W on T —5C 18
Hollybank Clo. Hamp —2F 13
Holly Bush La. Hamp —4E 12
Hollybush Rd. King T —2F 15
Holly Clo. Felt —2D 12
Hollyfield Rd. Surb —4G 21
Holly Ho. Iswth —3D 2
Hollymoor La. Eps —6K 25
Holly Rd. W4 —1A 4
Holly Rd. Hamp —3H 13
Holly Rd. Houn —1G 7
Holly Rd. Twic —5A 8
Holly Tree Clo. SW19
    —5G 11
Holman Hunt Ho. W6 —2H 5
    (off Field Rd.)
Holman Rd. Eps —2K 25
Holmbush Rd. SW15 —3H 11
Holmesdale Av. SW14 —7J 3
Holmesdale Rd. Rich —5G 3
Holmesdale Rd. Tedd
    —3D 14
Holmes Rd. Twic —6A 8
Holmoak Clo. SW15 —3J 11
Holmsley Clo. N Mald
    —3C 22
Holmwood Rd. Chess
    —2E 24
Holne Chase. Mord —3J 23
Holroyd Clo. Clay —5A 24
Holroyd Rd. SW15 —1F 11
Holroyd Rd. Clay —5A 24

Holsworthy Way. Chess
—2D **24**
Holwood Clo. W on T —6B **18**
Holybourne Av. SW15
—4D **10**
Holyport Rd. SW6 —4G **5**
Home Ct. Felt —5A **6**
Home Farm Clo. Th Dit
—7F **23**
Home Farm Gdns. W on T
—6B **18**
Homefield Rd. SW19 —3H **17**
Homefield Rd. W4 —1C **4**
Homefield Rd. W on T
—4D **18**
Home Pk. Rd. SW19 —1J **17**
Home Pk. Wlk. King T
—1E **20**
Homersham Rd. King T
—6H **15**
Homestead Rd. SW6 —4J **5**
Homewood Clo. Hamp
—3E **12**
Honeywood Rd. Iswth —1B **8**
Hood Av. SW14 —2K **9**
Hood Rd. SW20 —4C **16**
Hookfield. Eps —2K **27**
Hook Rise Bus. Cen. Chess
—7H **21**
Hook Rise N. Surb —7F **21**
Hook Rise S. Surb —7F **21**
Hook Rd. Chess & Surb
—2E **24**
Hook Rd. Eps —4K **25**
Hoppingwood Av. N Mald
—7B **16**
Hopton Gdns. N Mald
—3D **22**
Horace Rd. King T —7G **15**
Horder Rd. SW6 —5H **5**
Hornbeam Cres. Bren —4C **2**
Hornbeam Wlk. Rich —1G **15**
Horndon Clo. SW15 —5D **10**
Horne Way. SW15 —6F **5**
Horse Fair. King T —6E **14**
Horsley Clo. Eps —2K **27**
Horticultural Pl. W4 —2A **4**
Horton Footpath. Eps —7K **25**
Horton Gdns. Eps —7K **25**
Horton Hill. Eps —7K **25**
Horton Ho. W6 —2H **5**
(off Field Rd.)
Horton La. Eps —7H **25**
Hospital Bri. Rd. Twic —4G **7**
Hospital Rd. Houn —1F **7**
Hotham Clo. W Mol —7F **13**
Hotham Rd. SW15 —7F **5**
Houblon Rd. Rich —2F **9**
Houghton Clo. Hamp —3D **12**
Hounslow Av. Houn —2G **7**
Hounslow Bus. Pk. Houn
—1F **7**
Hounslow Gdns. Houn —2G **7**
Hounslow Rd. Felt —5A **6**
Hounslow Rd. Hanw —1C **12**
Hounslow Rd. Twic —3G **7**
Houston Pl. Esh —5J **19**
Howard Clo. Asht —7G **27**
Howard Clo. Hamp —4H **13**
Howard Rd. Iswth —7A **2**
Howard Rd. N Mald —7B **16**
Howard Rd. Surb —3G **21**
Howard's La. SW15 —1E **10**
Howard St. Th Dit —4C **20**
Howden Ho. Houn —4D **6**
Howgate Rd. SW14 —4A **4**
Howsman Rd. SW13 —3D **4**
Howson Ter. Rich —3F **9**
Hugh Dalton Ho. SW6 —3J **5**
(off Clem Attlee Ct.)
Hughenden Rd. Wor Pk
—4D **22**
Hugh Gaitskell Ho. SW6
(off Clem Attlee Ct.) —3J **5**
Hugon Rd. SW6 —7K **5**
Humbolt Rd. W6 —3H **5**

Hunston Rd. Mord —5K **23**
Hunter Rd. SW20 —5F **17**
Hunters Clo. Eps —2K **27**
Hunters Ct. Rich —2E **8**
Hunter's Rd. Chess —7F **21**
Huntingdon Gdns. W4 —4K **3**
Huntingdon Gdns. Wor Pk
—7F **23**
Huntingfield Rd. SW15
—1D **10**
Hunting Ga. Dri. Chess
—4F **25**
Hunting Ga. M. Twic —5K **7**
Huntley Way. SW20 —6D **16**
Huntsmans Clo. Felt —1A **12**
Huntsmoor Rd. Eps —2K **25**
Hurley Clo. W on T —6A **18**
Hurlingham Bus. Pk. SW6
—7K **5**
Hurlingham Ct. SW6 —7J **5**
Hurlingham Gdns. SW6
—7J **5**
Hurlingham Rd. SW6 —6J **5**
Hurlingham Sq. SW6 —7K **5**
Hurstbourne. Clay —3A **24**
Hurst Clo. Chess —2H **25**
Hurstcourt Rd. Sutt —6K **23**
Hurstfield Rd. W Mol —7F **13**
Hurst La. E Mol —1H **19**
Hurst Rd. Eps —7K **25**
Hurst Rd. W on T & W Mol
—2B **18**
Hurtwood Rd. W on T
—4E **18**
Hyacinth Clo. Hamp —3F **13**
Hyacinth Rd. SW15 —5D **10**
Hyde Rd. Rich —2G **9**
Hyde Wlk. Mord —4K **23**
Hylands Clo. Eps —4K **27**
Hylands M. Eps —4K **27**
Hylands Rd. Eps —4K **27**

Ibis La. W4 —5K **3**
Ibsley Gdns. SW15 —5D **10**
Idmiston Rd. Wor Pk —4C **22**
Idmiston Sq. Wor Pk —4C **22**
Iffley Rd. W6 —1E **4**
Ilex Clo. Sun —6B **12**
Imber Clo. Esh —5J **19**
Imber Ct. Trading Est. E Mol
—3J **19**
Imber Cross. Th Dit —3A **20**
Imber Gro. Esh —4J **19**
Imber Pk. Rd. Esh —5J **19**
Inglethorpe St. SW6 —5G **5**
Ingress St. W4 —2B **4**
Inkerman Ter. W8 —1K **5**
(off Allen St.)
Inner Pk. Rd. SW19 —5G **11**
Inner Staithe. W4 —5K **3**
Innes Clo. SW20 —6H **17**
Innes Gdns. SW15 —3E **10**
Interface Ho. Houn —1F **7**
(off Staines Rd.)
Inveresk Gdns. Wor Pk
—7C **22**
Inverness Rd. Houn —1E **6**
Inverness Rd. Wor Pk
—5G **23**
Inwood Av. Houn —1H **7**
Inwood Bus. Cen. Houn
—1G **7**
Inwood Ct. W on T —6B **18**
Inwood Rd. Houn —1G **7**
Irene Rd. SW6 —1K **5**
Iris Clo. Surb —4G **21**
Iris Rd. Eps —2J **25**
Isabella Ct. Rich —3G **9**
Isis Clo. SW15 —1F **11**
Isis Ct. W4 —4J **3**
Island Farm Av. W Mol
—2E **18**
Island Farm Rd. W Mol
—2E **18**
Island, The. Th Dit —3B **20**

Islay Gdns. Houn —2C **6**
Isleworth Bus. Complex. Iswth
—6A **2**
Isleworth Promenade. Twic
—1C **8**
Ivatt Pl. W14 —2J **5**
Ivybridge Clo. Twic —4B **8**
Ivy Clo. Sun —6B **12**
Ivy Cres. W4 —1K **3**
Ivydene. W Mol —2E **18**
Ivy La. Houn —1E **6**
Ivy Rd. Houn —1G **7**
Ivy Rd. Surb —5H **21**

James's Cotts. Rich —4H **3**
James St. Houn —1J **7**
Jasmine Dri. SW19 —2K **17**
Jasmine Way. E Mol —1K **19**
Jasmin Rd. Eps —2J **25**
Jefferson Clo. W13 —1C **2**
Jeffs Clo. Hamp —3G **13**
Jenner Pl. SW13 —3E **4**
Jeptha Rd. SW18 —3K **11**
Jerdan Pl. SW6 —4K **5**
Jersey Rd. Iswth —3A **2**
Jillian Clo. Hamp —4F **13**
Jim Griffiths Ho. SW6 —3J **5**
(off Clem Attlee Ct.)
Jocelyn Rd. Rich —7F **3**
Johnsons Dri. Hamp —5H **13**
John Wesley Ct. Twic —5B **8**
Jones M. SW15 —1H **11**
Jones Wlk. Rich —3G **9**
Jonquil Gdns. Hamp —3F **13**
Jordans Clo. Iswth —5A **2**
Joseph Locke Way. Esh
—6F **19**
Jubilee Av. Twic —5H **7**
Jubilee Clo. King T —5D **14**
Jubilee Way. Chess —1H **25**
Julien Rd. W5 —1D **2**
Junction Rd. W5 —1D **2**
Justin Clo. Bren —4E **2**

Katherine Rd. Twic —4B **8**
Kathleen Godfree Ct. SW19
—2K **17**
Keble Clo. Wor Pk —5C **22**
Kedeston Ct. Sutt —5K **23**
Keep, The. King T —3G **15**
Keevil Dri. SW19 —4G **11**
Kelso Rd. Cars —4K **23**
Kelvedon Clo. King T —3H **15**
Kelvedon Rd. SW6 —4J **5**
Kelvinbrook. W Mol —7G **13**
Kelvin Clo. Eps —3H **25**
Kelvin Ct. Iswth —6A **2**
Kelvin Dri. Twic —3C **8**
Kelvin Gro. Chess —7E **20**
Kempsford Gdns. SW5 —2K **5**
Kempson Rd. SW6 —5K **5**
Kempton Av. Sun —5A **12**
Kempton Ct. Sun —5A **12**
Kempton Rd. Hamp —6E **12**
Kendall Rd. Iswth —6B **2**
Kendal Pl. SW15 —2J **11**
Kendor Av. Eps —7K **25**
Kendrey Gdns. Twic —4K **7**
Kenilworth Av. SW19 —2K **17**
Kenilworth Dri. W on T
—7C **18**
Kenley Rd. SW19 —6K **17**
Kenley Rd. King T —6J **15**
Kenley Rd. Twic —3C **8**
Kenmore Clo. Rich —4H **3**
Kennet Rd. Iswth —7A **2**
Kennett Cl. W4 —4J **3**
Kensington Hall Gdns. W14
—2J **5**
Kensington High St. W14 &
W8 —1J **5**
Kent Dri. Tedd —5K **7**
Kent Ho. W4 —2B **4**
(off Devonshire Rd.)

Kenton Av. Sun —6C **12**
Kenton Ct. W14 —1J **5**
Kent Rd. W4 —1K **3**
Kent Rd. E Mol —1H **19**
Kent Rd. King T —7E **14**
Kent Rd. Rich —4H **3**
Kent's Pas. Hamp —5E **12**
Kent Way. Surb —7F **21**
Kentwode Grn. SW13 —4D **4**
Kenway Rd. SW5 —1K **5**
Kenwyn Rd. SW20 —5F **17**
Kenyngton Ct. Sun —2A **12**
Kenyngton Dri. Sun —2A **12**
Kenyon St. SW6 —5G **5**
Kersfield Rd. SW15 —3G **11**
Keswick Av. SW15 —2B **16**
Keswick Av. SW19 —6K **17**
Keswick Rd. SW15 —2H **11**
Keswick Rd. Twic —3H **7**
Kew Bri. Bren & Kew —3G **3**
Kew Bri. Arches. Rich —3H **3**
Kew Bri. Ct. W4 —2H **3**
Kew Bri. Rd. Bren —3G **3**
Kew Cres. Sutt —7H **23**
Kew Foot Rd. Rich —1F **9**
Kew Gdns. Rd. Rich —4G **3**
Kew Grn. Rich —3G **3**
Kew Meadow Path. Rich
—5J **3**
Kew Rd. Rich —3H **3**
Keynsham Rd. Mord —5K **23**
Killick Ho. Sutt —7K **23**
Kilmaine Rd. SW6 —4H **5**
Kilmarsh Rd. W6 —1F **5**
Kilmington Rd. SW13 —3D **4**
Kilmorey Gdns. Twic —2C **8**
Kilmorey Rd. Twic —1C **8**
Kilnside. Clay —4B **24**
Kilsha Rd. W on T —3B **18**
Kimball Gdns. SW6 —5H **5**
Kimberley Wlk. W on T
—4A **18**
Kimber Rd. SW18 —4K **11**
Kimpton Ind. Est. Sutt
—6J **23**
Kimpton Rd. Sutt —6J **23**
King Charles Cres. Surb
—4G **21**
King Charles Rd. Surb
—2G **21**
King Charles Wlk. SW19
—5H **11**
King Edward Dri. Chess
—7F **21**
King Edward M. SW13
—5D **4**
King Edwards Gro. Tedd
—3C **14**
King Edwards Mans. SW6
(off Fulham Rd.) —4K **5**
Kingfisher Ct. SW19 —6G **11**
Kingfisher Dri. Rich —1C **14**
King George Av. W on T
—5C **18**
King George Sq. Rich —3G **9**
King George's Trading Est.
Chess —1H **25**
King Henry's Rd. King T
—7J **15**
King's Arms All. Bren —3E **2**
Kings Av. N Mald —1B **22**
Kingsbridge Rd. Mord
—4G **23**
Kingsbridge Rd. W on T
—4A **18**
Kingsbrook. Lea —7B **26**
Kings Chase. E Mol —7H **13**
Kingsclere Clo. SW15
—4D **10**
Kingscliffe Gdns. SW19
—5J **11**
Kings Clo. W on T —6B **18**
Kingscote Rd. W4 —1A **4**
Kingscote Rd. N Mald —7A **16**
Kings Ct. W6 —1D **4**
(off King St.)

Kingsdowne Rd. Surb
Kings Dri. Surb —4H **2**
Kings Dri. Tedd —2J **13**
Kings Dri. Th Dit —3C **2**
Kings Farm Av. Rich —
Kingsgate Rd. King T —
Kingshill Av. Wor Pk —
Kings Keep. King T —1
Kingslawn Clo. SW15 —
Kingsley Ct. Wor Pk —
(off Avenue, The)
Kingsley Dri. Wor Pk —
Kings Mall. W6 —1F **5**
Kings Mead. Rich —3G
Kingsmead Av. Sun —
Kingsmead Av. Surb —
Kingsmead Av. Wor Pk
Kingsmead Clo. Tedd —
Kingsmeadow. King T
Kings Mead Pk. Clay —
Kingsmere Clo. SW15 —
Kingsmere Rd. SW19
—
Kingsnympton Pk. King
King's Paddock. Hamp
King's Pas. King T —6E
King's Pl. W4 —2K **3**
Kings Ride Ga. Rich —1
Kingsridge. SW19 —6H
Kings Rd. SW14 —7A **4**
Kings Rd. SW19 —3K **1**
Kings Rd. Felt —5B **6**
King's Rd. King T —5F **5**
Kings Rd. Rich —3G **9**
King's Rd. Surb —5D **2**
King's Rd. Tedd —2J **13**
King's Rd. Twic —3C **8**
King's Rd. W on T —6A
King's Ter. Iswth —1B **8**
Kingston Av. Sutt —7A **2**
Kingston Bri. King T —
Kingston By-Pass. Surb
SW20 —
Kingston By-Pass. Surb
N Mald
Kingston By-Pass Rd. Es
Surb —
Kingston Clo. Tedd —3C
Kingston Hall Rd. King **1**
Kingston Hill. King T —
Kingston Hill Pl. King T
Kingston Ho. Est. Surb
Kingston La. Tedd —2B
Kingston Rd. SW15 —6
Kingston Rd. SW20 & S
Kingston Rd. King T & N
Kingston Rd. Surb & Wc
—
Kingston Rd. Tedd —
Kingston Vale. SW15 —
King St. W6 —1D **4**
King St. Rich —2E **8**
King St. Twic —5B **8**
King's Wlk. King T —1E
Kingsway. SW14 —7J **3**
Kingsway. N Mald —2F
Kingsway Bus. Pk. Hamp
—
Kingswood Av. Hamp
Kingswood Clo. N Mald
Kingswood Clo. Surb —
Kingswood Rd. SW19
Kingswood Rd. W4 —1H

worthy Clo. King T
—7G **15**
od Rd. SW6 —5H **5**
rd Av. W4 —4K **3**
I Rd. W6 —3H **5**
s Av. Wor Pk —6D **22**
Way. W on T —3B **18**
s Rd. Surb —5F **21**
Rd. SW19 —5K **17**
d Rd. Mord —5K **23**
Clo. W4 —1A **4**
Rd. SW13 —5D **4**
borough Pl. SW5
—1K **5**
borough Pl. SW5
—1K **5**
' Gdns. Iswth —3J **7**
' Rd. N Mald —4B **22**
Rd. Twic —3H **7**
s Ct. King T —7F **15**
s Pk. King T —7F **15**
wood Cres. N Mald
—3B **22**
Rd. SW6 —3K **5**
ead. Surb —5K **21**
Clo. Wor Pk —7E **22**
Rd. Twic —5K **7**
r M. SW5 —2K **5**
I Wlk. Rich —3G **3**

num Cres. Sun —5A **12**
um Gro. Houn —1E **6**
um Gro. N Mald
—6A **16**
Dri. Hamp —5E **12**
Rd. SW15 —1G **11**
stile Ride. King T
—2J **15**
Booth Rd. King T
—6F **15**
lay. Wor Pk —6C **22**
ood Rd. Surb —6H **21**
Av. Felt —6B **6**
n St. SW18 —4K **11**
dns. Rich —6C **8**
Rd. SW19 —2J **17**
Pl. SW15 —3J **11**
St. SW6 —6H **5**
ert Av. Rich —7H **3**
ert Lodge. Bren —2E **2**
(Layton Rd.)
erts Rd. Surb —2G **21**
burne Av. SW19
—1J **17**
urn Gro. King T
—6J **15**
Pas. Bren —3G **3**
ook Ter. SW6 —5H **5**
ood Rd. SW20 —5F **17**
gton St. W6 —1E **4**
as Rd. Rich —1D **14**
ter Sq. W6 —3H **5**
on Ho. Clo. SW19
—1G **17**
on Rd. Houn —1G **7**
ster Av. SW19 —2G **17**
ster Clo. King T —2E **14**
ster Cotts. Rich —3F **9**
ster Ct. SW6 —4J **5**
ster Ct. W on T —4A **18**
ster Gdns. SW19
—2H **17**
ster Gdns. King T
—2E **14**
ster M. Rich —3F **9**
ster Pk. Rich —2F **9**
ster Pl. SW19 —2G **17**
ster Pl. Twic —3B **8**
ster Rd. SW19 —2G **17**
ord Rd. SW15 —7F **5**
rove Rd. SW19
—2K **17**
dge Rd. SW6 —6J **5**
eer Rd. N Mald —4A **22**
End. Eps —3J **27**

Laneway. SW15 —2E **10**
Lanfrey Pl. W14 —2J **5**
Langbourne Way. Clay
—3B **24**
Langdale Clo. SW14 —1J **9**
Langdon Pl. SW14 —7K **3**
Langham Gdns. Rich —1D **14**
Langham Ho. Clo. Rich
—1E **14**
*Langham Mans. SW5 —2K **5**
(off Earl's Ct. Sq.)*
Langham Pl. W4 —3B **4**
Langham Rd. SW20 —5F **17**
Langham Rd. Tedd —2C **14**
Langlands Rise. Eps —2K **27**
Langley Av. Surb —5E **20**
Langley Av. Wor Pk —6G **23**
Langley Gro. N Mald —6B **16**
Langley Rd. SW19 —5J **17**
Langley Rd. Iswth —6A **2**
Langley Rd. Surb —4F **21**
Langport Ct. W on T —5B **18**
Langside Av. SW15 —1D **10**
Langthorne St. SW6 —4G **5**
Langton Rd. W Mol —1H **19**
Langwood Chase. Tedd
—3D **14**
Lanigan Dri. Houn —2G **7**
*Lannoy Point. SW6 —4H **5**
(off Pellant Rd.)*
Lansbury Av. Felt —3A **6**
Lansdown Clo. W on T
—5B **18**
Lansdowne Clo. SW20
—4G **17**
Lansdowne Clo. Twic —5A **8**
Lansdowne Ct. Wor Pk
—6D **22**
Lansdowne Rd. SW20
—4F **17**
Lansdowne Rd. Eps —4K **25**
Lantern Clo. SW15 —1D **10**
Lapwing Ct. Surb —7H **21**
Lara Clo. Chess —4F **25**
Larch Cres. Eps —3J **25**
Larch Dri. W4 —2H **3**
Larches Av. SW14 —1A **10**
Largewood Av. Surb —6H **21**
Larkfield Rd. Rich —3F **9**
Larkspur Way. Eps —2K **25**
Larnach Rd. W6 —3G **5**
Larpent Av. SW15 —2F **11**
Latchmere Clo. Rich —2F **15**
Latchmere La. King T
—3G **15**
Latchmere Rd. King T
—4F **15**
Lateward Rd. Bren —3E **2**
Latham Clo. Twic —4B **8**
Latham Rd. Twic —4A **8**
Latimer Clo. Wor Pk —7E **22**
Latimer Rd. SW19 —3K **17**
Latimer Rd. Tedd —2A **14**
Latton Clo. Esh —7G **19**
Latton Clo. W on T —4D **18**
Latymer Ct. W6 —1G **5**
Lauderdale Dri. Rich —7E **8**
Laundry Rd. W6 —3H **5**
Laurel Av. Twic —5A **8**
Laurel Bank Gdns. SW6
—6J **5**
Laurel Gdns. Houn —1D **6**
Laurel Rd. SW13 —6D **4**
Laurel Rd. SW20 —5E **16**
Laurel Rd. Hamp —2J **13**
Lauriston Rd. SW19 —3G **17**
Lavender Av. Wor Pk —7F **23**
Lavender Ct. Felt —3A **6**
Lavender Ct. W Mol —7G **13**
Lavender Rd. Eps —2J **25**
Lavenham Rd. SW18 —6J **11**
Laverstoke Gdns. SW15
—4C **10**
Lawford Rd. W4 —4K **3**
Lawn Clo. N Mald —6B **16**
Lawn Cres. Rich —6H **3**

Lawns, The. SW19 —2J **17**
Lawrence Av. N Mald —3A **22**
Lawrence Rd. W5 —1D **2**
Lawrence Rd. Hamp —4E **12**
Lawrence Rd. Houn —1B **6**
Lawrence Rd. Rich —1D **14**
Lawrence Weaver Clo. Mord
—3K **23**
Lawson Clo. SW19 —7G **11**
Lawson Ct. Surb —4D **20**
Layton Ct. Bren —2E **2**
Layton Rd. Bren —2E **2**
Layton Rd. Houn —1G **7**
Leaf Clo. Th Dit —2K **19**
Leafield Rd. SW20 —7J **17**
Leafield Rd. Sutt —6K **23**
Leamington Av. Mord
—1H **23**
Leamington Clo. Houn —2H **7**
Leamore St. W6 —1F **5**
Leander Ct. Surb —4E **20**
Leas Clo. Chess —4G **25**
Leatherhead Rd. Asht —7F **27**
Leatherhead Rd. Chess
—3C **26**
Lebanon Av. Felt —2C **12**
Lebanon Gdns. SW18
—3K **11**
Lebanon Pk. Twic —4C **8**
Lebanon Rd. SW18 —2K **11**
Leconfield Av. SW13 —7C **4**
Leeson Ho. Twic —4C **8**
Leeward Gdns. SW19
—2H **17**
Legion Ct. Mord —3K **23**
Leicester Clo. Wor Pk —7F **23**
Leigham Dri. Iswth —4A **2**
Leigh Clo. N Mald —1A **22**
Leigh Rd. Houn —1J **7**
Leinster Av. SW14 —7K **3**
Lena Gdns. W6 —1F **5**
Lenelby Rd. Surb —5H **21**
Lenton Rise. Rich —7F **3**
Leo Ct. Bren —4E **2**
Leopold Av. SW19 —2J **17**
Leopold Rd. SW19 —1J **17**
Letterstone Rd. SW6 —4J **5**
Lettice St. SW6 —5J **5**
Levana Clo. SW19 —5H **11**
Lewesdon Clo. SW19
—5G **11**
Lewin Rd. SW14 —7A **4**
Lewins Rd. Eps —3J **27**
Lewis Rd. Rich —2E **8**
Lexham Gdns. W8 —1K **5**
Lexham M. W8 —1K **5**
Leybourne Pk. Rich —5H **3**
Leybourne Pk. Rich —5H **3**
Leyfield. Wor Pk —5B **22**
Library Way. Twic —4H **7**
Lichfield Gdns. Rich —1F **9**
Lichfield Rd. Houn —1B **6**
Lichfield Rd. Rich —5G **3**
*Lickey Ho. W14 —3J **5**
(off N. End Rd.)*
Liffords Pl. SW13 —6C **4**
Lifford St. SW15 —1G **11**
Lightcliffe Rd. Lea —7B **26**
Lily Clo. W14 —1G **5**
(in two parts)
Lilyville Rd. SW6 —5J **5**
Lime Cres. Sun —6B **12**
Lime Gro. N Mald —7A **16**
Lime Gro. Twic —3A **8**
Lime Rd. Rich —1G **9**
Limes Av. SW13 —6C **4**
Limes Field Rd. SW14 —7B **4**
Limes Gdns. SW18 —3K **11**
Limes, The. W Mol —1G **19**
Lime Tree Av. Esh & Th Dit
—5K **19**

Lime Tree Ct. Asht —7F **27**
Limpsfield Av. SW19 —6G **11**
Lincoln Av. SW19 —7G **11**
Lincoln Av. Twic —6H **7**
Lincoln Rd. Felt —7E **6**
Lincoln Rd. N Mald —7K **15**
Lincoln Rd. Wor Pk —6D **22**
Linden Av. Houn —2G **7**
Linden Clo. Th Dit —4A **20**
Linden Cres. King T —6G **15**
Linden Gdns. W4 —2B **4**
Linden Gro. N Mald —7B **16**
Linden Gro. Tedd —2A **14**
Linden Ho. Hamp —4F **13**
Lindens, The. W4 —5K **3**
Lindisfarne Rd. SW20
—4D **16**
Lindley Ct. King T —5D **14**
Lindley Rd. W on T —7C **18**
Lindsay Clo. Chess —4F **25**
Lindsay Clo. Eps —2K **27**
Lindsay Rd. Hamp —1G **13**
Lindsay Rd. Wor Pk —6E **22**
Lindum Rd. Tedd —4D **14**
Lingfield Av. King T —1F **21**
Lingfield Rd. SW19 —2G **17**
Lingfield Rd. Wor Pk —7F **23**
Linkenholt Mans. W6 —1C **4**
(off Stamford Brook Av.)
Linkfield. W Mol —7G **13**
Linkfield Rd. Iswth —6A **2**
Links Av. Mord —1K **23**
Links Clo. Asht —6D **26**
Linkside. N Mald —6B **16**
Links Pl. Asht —6E **26**
Links Rd. Asht —7D **26**
Links, The. W on T —6A **18**
Links View Rd. Hamp
—2H **13**
Linkway. SW20 —7E **16**
Linkway. Rich —6C **8**
Linslade Clo. Houn —2D **6**
Linstead Way. SW18 —4H **11**
Lintaine Clo. W6 —3H **5**
Linver Rd. SW6 —6K **5**
Lion Av. Twic —5A **8**
Lionel Rd. Bren —1F **3**
(in two parts)
Liongate M. E Mol —7A **14**
Lion Pk. Av. Chess —1H **25**
Lion Rd. Twic —5A **8**
Lion Way. Bren —4E **2**
Lion Wharf Rd. Iswth —7C **2**
Lisbon Av. Twic —6H **7**
Lisgar Ter. W14 —1J **5**
Lismore Clo. Iswth —6B **2**
Listergate Ct. SW15 —1E **11**
Litchfield Av. Mord —4J **23**
Littlecombe Clo. SW15
—3G **11**
Littlecote Clo. SW19 —4H **11**
Lit. Ealing La. W5 —1D **2**
Lit. Ferry Rd. Twic —5C **8**
Littlefield Clo. King T —6F **15**
Little Grn. Rich —1E **8**
Lit. Park Dri. Felt —6D **6**
Lit. Queen's Rd. Tedd
—3A **14**
Lit. St Leonard's. SW14
—7K **3**
Lit. Warkworth Ho. Iswth
—6C **2**
Littlewood Clo. W13 —1C **2**
Littleworth Comn. Rd. Esh
—7J **19**
Littleworth La. Esh —7J **19**
Littleworth Pl. Esh —7J **19**
Littleworth Rd. Esh —7K **19**
Liverpool Rd. King T —4H **15**
Livingstone Rd. Houn —1H **7**
Lloyd Rd. Wor Pk —7G **23**
Lochaline St. W6 —3F **5**
Lockesley Sq. Surb —3E **20**
Lock Rd. Rich —1D **14**

Locksmeade Rd. Rich
—1D **14**
Lockwood Way. Chess
—2H **25**
Lodge Av. SW14 —7B **4**
Lodge Clo. Iswth —5C **2**
Logan Clo. Houn —1E **6**
Logan M. W8 —1K **5**
Logan Pl. W8 —1K **5**
London Rd. Bren —4C **2**
London Rd. Iswth —6A **2**
London Rd. King T —6F **15**
London Rd. Mord —2K **23**
London Rd. Sutt —7F **23**
London Rd. Twic —2B **8**
London Stile. W4 —2H **3**
Longfellow Rd. Wor Pk
—5D **22**
Longfield Dri. SW14 —2J **9**
Longfield St. SW18 —4K **11**
Longford Clo. Hamp —1F **13**
Longford Ct. Eps —1K **25**
Longford Ho. Hamp —1F **13**
Longford Rd. Twic —5F **7**
Long Gro. Rd. Eps —6J **25**
Long Lodge Dri. W on T
—7B **18**
Longmead Rd. Th Dit
—4K **19**
Longridge Rd. SW5 —1K **5**
Longs Ct. Rich —1G **9**
Longstaff Cres. SW18
—4K **11**
Longstaff Rd. SW18 —3K **11**
Long Wlk. SW13 —6C **4**
Long Wlk. N Mald —7K **15**
Longwood Dri. SW15
—3D **10**
Lonsdale Ct. Surb —6E **20**
Lonsdale M. Rich —5H **3**
Lonsdale Rd. SW13 —5C **4**
Lonsdale Rd. W4 —1C **4**
Loop Rd. Eps —5K **27**
Loraine Gdns. Asht —6F **27**
Loraine Rd. W4 —3J **3**
Lord Chancellor Wlk. King T
—5A **16**
Lord Napier Pl. W6 —2D **4**
Lord Roberts M. SW6 —4K **5**
Lords Clo. Felt —6D **6**
Loring Rd. Iswth —6A **2**
Lorne Rd. Rich —2G **9**
Louisa Ct. Twic —6K **7**
Lovekyn Clo. King T —6F **15**
Lovelace Gdns. Surb —4E **20**
Lovelace Rd. Surb —4D **20**
Love La. Mord —4K **23**
Love La. Surb —6D **20**
Lovell Rd. Rich —7D **8**
Lovett Dri. Cars —4K **23**
Lwr. Common S. SW15
—7E **4**
Lwr. Court Rd. Eps —7K **25**
Lwr. Downs Rd. SW20
—5G **17**
Lwr. George St. Rich —1F **9**
Lwr. Green Rd. Esh —6G **19**
Lwr. Grove Rd. Rich —3G **9**
Lwr. Hampton Rd. Sun
—7B **12**
Lwr. Ham Rd. King T —4D **14**
Lwr. Hill Rd. Eps —1J **27**
Lwr. Mall. W6 —2E **4**
Lwr. Marsh La. King T
—1G **21**
Lwr. Morden La. Mord
—3F **23**
Lwr. Mortlake Rd. Rich —1F **9**
Lwr. Richmond Rd. SW14 &
SW15 —7E **4**
Lwr. Richmond Rd. Rich &
SW14 —7H **3**
Lwr. Sq. Iswth —7C **2**
Lwr. Staithe. W4 —5K **3**
Lwr. Sunbury Rd. Hamp
—6E **12**

Lwr. Teddington Rd. King T —5E 14
Lwr. Wood Rd. Clay —3C 24
Lowther Rd. SW13 —5C 4
Lowther Rd. King T —5G 15
Loxley Rd. Hamp —1E 12
Lucien Rd. SW19 —6K 11
Ludovick Wlk. SW15 —1C 10
Lurgan Av. W6 —3G 5
Lushington Ho. W on T
　—3B 18
Luther Rd. Tedd —2A 14
Luttrell Av. SW15 —2E 10
Luxemburg Gdns. W6 —1G 5
Lydney Clo. SW19 —6H 11
Lygon Ho. SW6 —5H 5
　(off Fulham Pal. Rd.)
Lymescote Gdns. Sutt
　—6K 23
Lyncroft Gdns. Houn —2H 7
Lynde Ho. W on T —3B 18
Lyndhurst Av. Surb —5J 21
Lyndhurst Av. Twic —5E 6
Lyndhurst Dri. N Mald
　—4B 22
Lynmouth Av. Mord —3G 23
Lynton Clo. Chess —1F 25
Lynton Clo. Iswth —1A 8
Lynton Rd. N Mald —2A 22
Lynwood Ct. King T —6J 15
Lynwood Dri. Wor Pk —6D 22
Lynwood Rd. Th Dit —6A 20
Lyon Rd. W on T —6D 18
Lyons Wlk. W14 —1H 5
Lyric Rd. SW13 —5C 4
Lysia St. SW6 —4G 5
Lysons Wlk. SW15 —1D 10
Lytcott Dri. W Mol —7E 12
Lytton Gro. SW15 —2G 11

Mablethorpe Rd. SW6
　—4H 5
Macaulay Av. Esh —6A 20
Macbeth St. W6 —2E 4
McCarthy Rd. Felt —2C 12
McDonough Clo. Chess
　—1F 25
Macfarlane La. Iswth —3A 2
McKay Rd. SW20 —4E 16
Maclaren M. SW15 —1F 11
Maclise Rd. W14 —1H 5
Madans Wlk. Eps —4K 27
Maddison Clo. Tedd —3A 14
Madrid Rd. SW13 —5D 4
Mafeking Av. Bren —3F 3
Magdala Rd. Iswth —7B 2
Magnolia Clo. King T —3J 15
Magnolia Rd. W4 —3J 3
Magnolia Way. Eps —2K 25
Maguire Dri. Rich —1D 14
Maidenshaw Rd. Eps —1K 27
Maids of Honour Row. Rich
　—2E 8
Main St. Felt —2C 12
Malbrook Rd. SW15 —1E 10
Malcolm Dri. Surb —5E 20
Malcolm Rd. SW19 —3H 17
Malden Ct. N Mald —7A 16
Malden Grn. Av. Wor Pk
　—5C 22
Malden Hill. N Mald —7C 16
Malden Hill Gdns. N Mald
　—7C 16
Malden Pk. N Mald —3C 22
Malden Rd. N Mald & Wor Pk
　—2B 22
Malden Rd. Sutt —7G 23
Malden Way. N Mald —3B 22
Mallard Clo. Twic —4F 7
Mallard Pl. Twic —7B 8
Mall Rd. W6 —2E 4
Mall, The. SW14 —2K 9
Mall, The. Bren —3E 2
Mall, The. Surb —3E 20
Maltby Rd. Chess —3H 25

Maltese Dri. Felt —2C 12
Maltings. W4 —2H 3
Maltings Clo. SW13 —6C 4
Malvern Clo. Surb —5F 21
Malvern Dri. Felt —2C 12
Malvern Rd. Hamp —4F 13
Malvern Rd. Surb —6F 21
Manbre Rd. W6 —3F 5
Mandeville Clo. SW20
　—5H 17
Mandeville Dri. Surb —5E 20
Mandeville Rd. Iswth —6B 2
Manfred Rd. SW15 —2J 11
Manningtree Clo. SW19
　—5H 11
Mann's Clo. Iswth —2A 8
Manoel Rd. Twic —7H 7
Manor Clo. Wor Pk —5B 22
Manor Ct. W3 —1H 3
Manor Ct. Twic —6H 7
Manor Ct. W Mol —1F 19
Manor Cres. Surb —3H 21
Manordene Clo. Th Dit
　—5B 20
Manor Dri. Esh —6A 20
Manor Dri. Felt —2C 12
Manor Dri. Surb —3G 21
Manor Dri. N. N Mald &
　Wor Pk —4A 22
Manor Dri., The. Wor Pk
　—5B 22
Manor Fields. SW15 —3G 11
Manor Gdns. SW20 —6J 17
Manor Gdns. W3 —1H 3
Manor Gdns. W4 —2B 4
Manor Gdns. Hamp —4G 13
Manor Gdns. Rich —1G 9
Manorgate Rd. King T —5H 15
Manor Grn. Rd. Eps —2J 27
Manor Gro. Rich —1H 9
Manor Ho. Ct. Eps —2K 27
Manor La. Felt —6A 6
Manor La. Sun —6A 12
Manor Pk. Rich —1G 9
Manor Pl. Felt —5A 6
Manor Rd. SW20 —6J 17
Manor Rd. E Mol —1J 19
Manor Rd. Rich —1H 9
Manor Rd. Tedd —2B 14
Manor Rd. Twic —6H 7
Manor Rd. N. Hin W & Th Dit
　—7A 20
Manor Rd. S. Esh —1A 24
Manor Vale. Bren —2D 2
Manor Way. Wor Pk —5B 22
Mansel Rd. SW19 —3H 17
Mansfield Rd. Chess —2D 24
Mansions, The. SW5 —2K 5
Maple Clo. Hamp —3E 12
Maple Ct. N Mald —7A 16
Maple Gro. Bren —4C 2
Maplehurst Clo. King T
　—1F 21
Maple Ind. Est. Felt —7A 6
Maple Rd. Asht —7E 26
Maple Rd. Surb —3C 20
Mapleton Cres. SW18 —3K 11
Mapleton Rd. SW18 —3K 11
　(in two parts)
Maple Way. Felt —7A 6
Marble Hill Clo. Twic —4C 8
Marble Hill Gdns. Twic —4C 8
Marchbank Rd. W14 —3J 5
Marchmont Rd. Rich —2G 9
March Rd. Twic —4B 8
Marco Rd. W6 —1F 5
Margin Dri. SW19 —2G 17
Margravine Gdns. W6 —2G 5
Margravine Rd. W6 —2G 5
Maria Theresa Clo. N Mald
　—2A 22
Marina Av. N Mald —2E 22
Marina Way. Tedd —4E 14
Mariner Gdns. Rich —7D 8
Market Pl. Bren —4D 2

Market Pl. King T —6E 14
Market Rd. Rich —7H 3
Market Ter. Bren —3F 3
　(off Albany Rd.)
Markhole Clo. Hamp —4E 12
Marksbury Av. Rich —7H 3
Markway. Sun —6B 12
Marlborough Clo. W on T
　—7C 18
Marlborough Cres. W4 —1A 4
Marlborough Gdns. Surb
　—4E 20
Marlborough Rd. W4 —2K 3
Marlborough Rd. Felt —6C 6
Marlborough Rd. Hamp
　—3F 13
Marlborough Rd. Iswth —5C 2
Marlborough Rd. Rich —3G 9
Marlborough Rd. Sutt —7K 23
Marld, The. Asht —7G 27
Marlingdene Clo. Hamp
　—3F 13
Marlow Cres. Twic —3A 8
Marlow Dri. Sutt —6G 23
Marnell Way. Houn —1C 6
Marneys Clo. Eps —4H 27
Marrick Clo. SW15 —1D 10
Marryat Pl. SW19 —1H 17
Marryat Rd. SW19 —2G 17
Marshall Clo. Houn —2E 6
Marshalls Clo. Eps —2K 27
Marsh Farm Rd. Twic —5A 8
Marston. Eps —7K 25
Marston Av. Chess —3F 25
Marston Ct. W on T —5B 18
Marston Rd. Tedd —2C 14
Martindale. SW14 —2K 9
Martindale Rd. Houn —1D 6
Martingales Clo. Rich —7E 8
Martin Gro. Mord —1K 23
Martin Way. SW20 & Mord
　—7H 17
Marville Rd. SW6 —4J 5
Mary Adelaide Clo. SW15
　—1B 16
Maryland Way. Sun —6A 12
Mary Macarthur Ho. W6
　—3H 5
Mary Rose Clo. Hamp —5F 13
Mary's Ter. Twic —4B 8
Marzena Ct. Houn —3H 7
Mascotte Rd. SW15 —1G 11
Masefield Ct. Surb —4E 20
Masefield Rd. Hamp —1E 12
Mason Clo. Hamp —5F 13
Masonettes. Eps —6K 25
　(off Sefton Rd.)
Mason's Yd. SW19 —2G 17
Maswell Pk. Cres. Houn
　—2H 7
Maswell Pk. Rd. Houn —2G 7
Matham Rd. E Mol —2J 19
Matheson Rd. W14 —1J 5
Mathias Clo. Eps —2K 27
Matlock Way. N Mald —5A 16
Maudsley Ho. Bren —4E 3
Maurice Ct. Bren —4E 2
Mawson Clo. SW20 —6H 17
Mawson La. W4 —3C 4
Maxwell Rd. SW6 —4K 5
Mayberry Pl. Surb —4G 21
May Clo. Chess —3G 25
Maycross Av. Mord —1J 23
Mayfair Av. Twic —4H 7
Mayfair Av. Wor Pk —5D 22
Mayfair Clo. Surb —5F 21
Mayfield. W4 —1B 4
Mayfield Clo. Th Dit —5C 20
Mayfield Clo. W on T —7A 18
Mayfield Rd. SW19 —5J 17
Mayfield Rd. W on T —7A 18
Mayo Ct. W13 —1C 2
May Rd. Twic —5K 7
Mayroyd Av. Surb —6H 21
Mays Rd. Tedd —2J 13
May St. W14 —2J 5

Maze Rd. Rich —4H 3
Meade Clo. W4 —3H 3
Mead End. Asht —6G 27
Meadlands Dri. Rich —6E 8
Meadowbank. Surb —3G 21
Meadowbank Clo. SW6 —4F 5
Meadow Clo. SW20 —1F 23
Meadow Clo. Esh —7A 20
Meadow Clo. Houn —4F 7
Meadow Clo. Rich —5F 9
Meadow Ct. Eps —2K 27
Meadow Ct. Houn —3J 7
Meadowcroft. W4 —2H 3
　(off Brooks La.)
Meadow Hill. N Mald —3B 22
Meadow Pl. W4 —4B 4
Meadow Rd. Asht —6F 27
Meadow Rd. Clay —3A 24
Meadow Rd. Felt —6D 6
Meadowside. Twic —4E 8
Meadowside. W on T —6B 18
Meadow Way. Chess —2F 25
Mead Rd. Rich —7D 8
Mead Rd. W on T —7D 18
Meads, The. Sutt —7H 23
Mead Way. SW20 —1F 23
Meadway. Eps —1K 27
Meadway. Surb —5K 21
Meadway. Twic —5J 7
Meadway Ct. Tedd —2D 14
Medcroft Gdns. SW14 —1K 9
Medfield St. SW15 —4D 10
Medina Av. Esh —2K 19
Melancholy Wlk. Rich —6D 8
Melbourne Rd. SW19 —5K 17
Melbourne Rd. Tedd —3D 14
Melbury Clo. Clay —3C 24
Melbury Gdns. SW20 —5D 16
Meldone Clo. Surb —3J 21
Melford Clo. Chess —2G 25
Melina Ct. SW15 —7D 4
Mellor Clo. W on T —4E 18
Melrose Av. SW19 —6J 11
Melrose Av. Twic —4G 7
Melrose Gdns. N Mald
　—7A 16
Melrose Rd. SW13 —6C 4
Melrose Rd. SW18 —3J 11
Melrose Rd. SW19 —5K 17
Melville Av. SW20 —4D 16
Melville Rd. SW13 —5D 4
Mendip Clo. SW19 —6H 11
Mendip Clo. Wor Pk —6F 23
Mendora Rd. SW6 —4H 5
Mercer Clo. Th Dit —4B 20
Mercers Pl. W6 —1F 5
Mercier Rd. SW15 —2H 11
Mercury Cen. Felt —2A 6
Mercury Ho. Bren —3D 2
　(off Glenhurst Rd.)
Mercury Rd. Bren —3D 2
Mere Clo. SW15 —4G 11
Meredyth Rd. SW13 —6D 4
Mereway Rd. Twic —5J 7
Merivale Rd. SW15 —1H 11
Merrilands Rd. Wor Pk
　—5F 23
Merrilyn Clo. Clay —3B 24
Merrington Rd. SW6 —3K 5
Merthyr Ter. SW13 —3E 4
Merton Av. W4 —1C 4
Merton Hall Gdns. SW20
　—5H 17
Merton Hall Rd. SW19
　—4H 17
Merton Mans. SW20 —6G 17
Merton Rd. SW18 —3K 11
Merton Rd. SW19 —4K 17
Merton Wlk. Lea —7B 26
Merton Way. Lea —7B 26
Merton Way. W Mol —1G 19
Metcalf Wlk. Felt —1D 12
Mews, The. Twic —3C 8
Mexfield Rd. SW15 —2J 11
Michael's Row. Rich —1F 9

Michael Stewart Ho. SW6
　(off Clem Attlee Ct.)
Michelham Gdns. Twic
Michel's Row. Rich —
Micklethwaite Rd. SW6
Midas Metropolitan Ind
　Mord —
Middle Grn. Clo. Surb
Middle La. Tedd —3A 1
Middlesex Ct. W4 —2C
Middleton Rd. Eps —6
Middleton Rd. Mord &
Middleton Rd. N Mald
Midmoor Rd. SW19 —
Midsummer Av. Houn
Midway. Sutt —4J 23
Midway. W on T —6A
Miena Way. Asht —
Miles Pl. Surb —1G 21
Millais Rd. N Mald —4
Millais Way. Eps —1K
Millbourne Rd. Felt —
Miller's Ct. W6 —2C 4
Millers Farm Cres. Houn
Millfield Rd. Houn —5[
Mill Hill Rd. SW13 —6
Mill Pl. King T —7G 15
Mill Plat. Iswth —6B 2
　(in two parts)
Mill Plat Av. Iswth —6
Mill Rd. Esh —6F 19
Mill Rd. Twic —6H 7
Mill Shot Clo. SW6 —
Millside Pl. Iswth —6C
Mills Row. W4 —1A 4
Mill St. King T —7F 15
Mill Way. Felt —2A 6
Millwood Rd. Houn —
Milner Dri. Twic —4J 7
Milner Rd. SW19 —5K
Milner Rd. King T —7E
Milnthorpe Rd. W4 —3
Milton Ct. Twic —7K 7
Milton Ho. Sutt —7K 2
Milton Lodge. Twic —
Milton Rd. SW14 —7A
Milton Rd. Hamp —4F
Milton Rd. Sutt —7K 2
Milton Rd. W on T —7
Mimosa St. SW6 —5J
Mina Rd. SW19 —5K 1
Minden Rd. Sutt —6J 2
Minerva Rd. King T —
Minniedale. Surb —2G
Minstead Gdns. SW15
Minstead Way. N Mald
Minster Av. Sutt —6K 2
Minster Gdns. W Mol —
Minstrel Gdns. Surb —
Mirabel Rd. SW6 —4J
Mission Sq. Bren —3F
Misty's Field. W on T —
Moat Ct. Asht —6F 27
Moatside. Felt —1B 12
Moat, The. N Mald —6
Modder Pl. SW15 —1G
Model Cotts. SW14 —1
Moffat Ct. SW19 —2K
Mogden La. Iswth —2A
Mole Abbey Gdns. W M
Mole Ct. Eps —1K 25
Molember Ct. E Mol —
Molember Rd. E Mol —
Molesey Av. W Mol —2
Molesey Clo. W on T —
Molesey Dri. Sutt —6H
Molesey Pk. Av. W Mol
Molesey Pk. Clo. E Mol

Pk. Rd. W Mol
—2G 19
Rd. W on T & W Mol
—7C 18
d Rd. SW6 —5K 5
n Clo. W Mol
—7G 13
in Way. W Mol
—7G 13
in Gdns. W Mol
—7G 13
h Rd. Mord —7H 17
v. W Mol —2E 18
res. W on T —5A 18
th Av. King T —4D 14
th Gro. Bren —1F 3
. Felt —6A 6
Dri. SW14 —2J 9
e Clo. W on T
—4A 18
e Rd. SW19 —4K 17
e Rd. Houn —1G 7
e Rd. Rich —3F 9
Rd. SW20 —5F 17
Rd. N Mald —1B 22
Rd. Sun —1A 18
Pl. SW19 —5G 11
nery Av. Esh —6K 19
nery Rd. W4 —1K 3
u Gdns. SW15
—2E 10
er Row. Twic —4G 7
e Av. Twic —4G 7
at Rd. SW15 —1H 11
. N Mald —2J 9
k. Rd. SW6 —4K 5
d Rd. Chess —2F 25
d Clo. Twic —4F 7
. Chess —1F 25
ead Rd. Twic —3B 8
. Gdns. King T
—4B 16
Ct. Mord —1K 23
Ct. Pde. Mord
—1K 23
Way. Sutt —4K 23
. W14 —1G 5
mbe Clo. King T
—4J 15
Esh —7G 19
Av. Surb —4J 21
Rd. Mor Pk —6D 22
Rd. Tedd —3K 13
Clo. Hamp —2E 12
d. Sutt —5J 23
td. Twic —3E 8
side Rd. Wor Pk
—6F 23
ton Av. W14 —1J 5
ton Wlk. Rich
—1D 14
dns. SW18 —4K 11
d. Iswth —7A 2
r Cres. Wor Pk
—7A 22
. High St. SW14
—7A 4
. Rd. Rich —4H 3
M. SW5 —1K 5
e Gdns. Mord —7J 17
Rd. SW19 —5J 17
Pk. N Mald —3C 22
elus Rd. SW15
—4C 10
at Rd. Rich —2F 9
mbe Clo. Surb
—4F 21
t. SW15 —7H 5
l. Hamp —5G 13
sant Rd. N Mald
—7K 15
td. SW19 —6K 11
td. Chess —2G 25
td. Felt —7D 6
td. N Mald —7A 16
The. N Mald —7C 16

Mt. View Rd. Clay —4C 24
Mount Wood. W Mol —7G 13
Mowat Clo. Wor Pk —6C 22
(off Avenue, The)
Mowbray Rd. Rich —7D 8
Moylan Rd. W6 —3H 5
Muirdown Av. SW14 —1A 10
Mulberry Ct. Surb —4E 20
Mulberry Ct. Twic —7A 8
Mulberry Cres. Bren —4C 2
Mulberry Pl. W6 —2D 4
Mulgrave Rd. SW6 —3J 5
Mullins Path. SW14 —7A 4
Munden St. W14 —1H 5
Mund St. W14 —2J 5
Munnings Gdns. Iswth —2J 7
Munster Av. Houn —2D 6
Munster Rd. SW6 —4H 5
Munster Rd. Tedd —3D 14
Murfett Clo. SW19 —6H 11
Murray Av. Houn —2G 7
Murray Ct. Twic —6J 7
Murray Rd. SW19 —3G 17
Murray Rd. W5 —1D 2
Murray Rd. Rich —6D 8
Murreys Ct. Asht —7E 26
Murreys, The. Asht —7E 26
Musard Rd. W6 —3H 5
Musgrave Cres. SW6 —4K 5
Musgrave Rd. Iswth —5A 2
Mustow Pl. SW6 —6J 5
Muybridge Rd. N Mald
—6K 15
Mylne Clo. W6 —2D 4
Mynn's Clo. Eps —3J 27
Myrtle Gro. N Mald —6K 15
Myrtle Rd. Hamp —3H 13

**N**
Nallhead Rd. Felt —2B 12
Napier Av. SW6 —7J 5
Napier Clo. SW6 —7J 5
(off Ranelagh Gdns.)
Napier Pl. W14 —1J 5
Napier Rd. W14 —1H 5
Napier Av. SW6 —7J 5
Napier Rd. Iswth —1B 8
Napoleon Rd. Twic —4C 8
Narborough St. SW6 —6K 5
Naseby Clo. Iswth —5A 2
Naseby Ct. W on T —6B 18
Nasmyth St. W6 —1E 4
Nassau Rd. SW13 —5C 4
Nella Rd. W6 —3G 5
Nelson Clo. W on T —5A 18
Nelson Gdns. Houn —3F 7
Nelson Ind. Est. SW19
—5K 17
Nelson Rd. Houn —3F 7
Nelson Rd. N Mald —2A 22
Nelson Rd. Twic —3F 7
Nene Gdns. Felt —6E 6
Nepean St. SW15 —3D 10
Nero Ct. Bren —4E 2
Netheravon Rd. W4 —1C 4
Netheravon Rd. S. W4 —2C 4
Netherbury Rd. W5 —1E 2
Netherton Rd. Twic —2B 8
Netley Dri. W on T —4E 18
Netley Rd. Bren —3F 3
Nevada Clo. N Mald —1K 21
Nevern Mans. SW5 —1K 5
(off Warwick Rd.)
Nevern Pl. SW5 —1K 5
Nevern Rd. SW5 —1K 5
Nevern Sq. SW5 —1K 5
Neville Av. N Mald —5A 16
Neville Gill Clo. SW18
—3K 11
Neville Rd. King T —6H 15
Neville Rd. Rich —7D 8
Newark Ct. W on T —5B 18
Newborough Grn. N Mald
—1A 22
New Broadway. Hamp
—2J 13
Newbury Gdns. Eps —7C 22

New Chapel Sq. Felt —5A 6
New Clo. Felt —2D 12
Newfield Clo. Hamp —5F 13
Newgate Clo. Felt —7D 6
Newhouse Clo. N Mald
—4B 22
New Kelvin Av. Tedd —3K 13
New Kings Rd. SW6 —6J 5
Newlands Av. Th Dit —5K 19
Newlands Way. Chess
—2D 24
Newmans La. Surb —3E 20
Newnes Path. SW15 —1E 10
Newport Rd. SW13 —5D 4
New Rd. Bren —3E 2
New Rd. Esh —7H 19
New Rd. Felt —5A 6
New Rd. Hanw —2D 12
New Rd. Houn —1G 7
New Rd. King T —4H 15
New Rd. Oxs —7A 24
New Rd. Rich —1D 14
New Rd. W Mol —1F 19
Newry Rd. Twic —2B 8
Newstead Wlk. Cars —4K 23
Newstead Way. SW19
—1G 17
Newton Gro. W4 —1B 4
Newton Rd. SW19 —4H 17
Newton Rd. Iswth —6A 2
Newton's Yd. SW18 —2K 11
Newton Wood Rd. Asht
—5G 27
Niagara Av. W5 —1D 2
Nicholes Rd. Houn —1F 7
Nicol Clo. Twic —3C 8
Nigel Playfair Av. W6 —2E 4
Nightingale Clo. W4 —3K 3
Nightingale Dri. Eps —3J 25
Nightingale La. Rich —4F 9
Nightingale Rd. Hamp —2F 13
Nightingale Rd. W on T
—4B 18
Nightingale Rd. W Mol
—2G 19
Nimbus Rd. Eps —6K 25
Niton Rd. Rich —7H 3
Niton St. SW6 —4G 5
Norbiton Av. King T —5H 15
Norbiton Comn. Rd. King T
—7J 15
Norbury Av. Houn —1J 7
Norcutt Rd. Twic —5K 7
Norfolk Clo. Twic —3C 8
Norfolk Gdns. Houn —2E 6
Norfolk Rd. Felt —5B 6
Norfolk Ter. W6 —2H 5
Norley Vale. SW15 —5D 10
Norman Av. Felt —6D 6
Norman Av. Twic —4D 8
Norman Colyer Ct. Eps
—6K 25
Normand M. W14 —3H 5
Normand Rd. W14 —3J 5
Normandy Clo. SW15 —2J 11
Norman Ho. Felt —6E 6
Normanhurst Dri. Twic —2B 8
Normanhurst Rd. W on T
—6C 18
Normansfield Av. Tedd
—4D 14
Normanton Av. SW19 —6K 11
Norroy Rd. SW15 —1G 11
Norstead Pl. SW15 —6D 10
North Av. Rich —5H 3
Northcliffe Clo. Wor Pk
—7B 22
North Clo. Mord —1H 23
Northcote Av. Iswth —2B 8
Northcote Av. Surb —4J 21
Northcote Rd. N Mald
—7K 15
Northcote Rd. Twic —2B 8
N. End Pde. W14 —1H 5
(off N. End Rd.)

N. End Rd. W14 & SW6
—1H 5
Northernhay Wlk. Mord
—1H 23
N. Eyot Gdns. W6 —2C 4
N. Feltham Trading Est. Felt
—2A 6
Northfield Av. W5 —1D 2
Northfields. SW18 —1K 11
Northfields. Asht —7F 27
Northfields Prospect Bus. Cen.
SW18 —1K 11
North La. Tedd —3A 14
North Pde. Chess —2G 25
North Pl. SW18 —2K 11
North Pl. Tedd —3A 14
North Rd. W5 —1E 2
North Rd. Bren —3F 3
North Rd. Rich —7H 3
North Rd. Surb —3E 20
Northspur Rd. Sutt —7K 23
North St. Iswth —2K 9
Northumberland Av. Iswth
—5A 2
Northumberland Gdns. Iswth
—4B 2
Northumberland Pl. Rich
—3E 8
Northumberland Row. Twic
—5K 7
N. Verbena Gdns. W6 —2D 4
North View. SW19 —2F 17
Northway. Mord —1H 23
N. Worple Way. SW14 —7A 4
Norton Av. Surb —4J 21
Nottingham Rd. Iswth —6A 2
Nova M. Sutt —5H 23
Novello St. SW6 —5K 5
Nowell Rd. SW13 —3D 4
Numa Ct. Bren —4E 2
Nursery Clo. SW15 —1G 11
Nursery Clo. Felt —4A 6
Nursery Rd. SW19 —4H 17
(Wimbledon)
Nylands Av. Rich —5H 3
Nymans Gdns. SW20 —7E 16

**O**
Oak Av. Hamp —2D 12
Oakbank Av. W on T —4E 18
Oakcombe Clo. N Mald
—5B 16
Oakcroft Bus. Cen. Chess
—1G 25
Oakcroft Rd. Chess —1G 25
Oakcroft Vs. Chess —1G 25
Oakdene Av. Th Dit —5B 20
Oakdene Dri. Surb —4K 21
Oakdene M. Sutt —5J 23
Oake Ct. SW15 —2H 11
Oaken Dri. Clay —3A 24
Oaken La. Clay —2A 24
Oakenshaw Clo. Surb —4F 21
Oakfield Clo. N Mald —2C 22
Oakfield Rd. SW19 —7G 11
Oakfield Rd. Asht —6E 26
Oakfield Rd. Th Dit —2A 20
Oakfields. W on T —5A 18
Oak Glade. Eps —1H 27
Oak Gro. Sun —4A 12
Oakhill. Clay —3B 24
Oak Hill. Eps —5K 27
Oakhill. Surb —4F 21
Oakhill Clo. Asht —7D 26
Oakhill Ct. SW19 —4G 17
Oakhill Cres. Surb —4F 21
Oakhill Dri. Surb —4F 21
Oakhill Gro. Surb —3F 21
Oakhill Path. Surb —3F 21
Oakhill Pl. SW15 —2K 11
Oakhill Rd. SW15 —2J 11
Oakhill Rd. Asht —7D 26
Oakhill Rd. Surb —3F 21
Oakhurst Clo. Tedd —2K 13
Oakhurst Rd. Eps —3K 25

Oakington Dri. Sun —6B 12
Oaklands Av. Esh —5J 19
Oaklands Av. Iswth —3A 2
Oaklands Clo. Chess —1D 24
Oaklands Dri. Twic —4H 7
Oaklands Rd. SW14 —7A 4
Oak La. Twic —4B 8
Oaklawn Rd. Lea —6A 26
Oak Leaf Clo. Eps —1K 27
Oaklea Pas. King T —7E 14
Oakleigh Av. Surb —5H 21
Oakleigh Way. Surb —5H 21
Oakley Wlk. W6 —3G 5
Oakmead Grn. Eps —4K 27
Oak Pk. Gdns. SW19 —5G 11
Oak Rd. Lea —7B 26
Oak Rd. N Mald —6A 16
Oaks Av. Felt —6D 6
Oaks Av. Wor Pk —7E 22
Oaksway. Surb —5E 20
Oak Way. SW20 —1F 23
Oak Way. Asht —5H 27
Oakwood Gdns. Sutt —6K 23
Oakwood Rd. SW20 —5D 16
Observatory Rd. SW14 —1K 9
Occupation La. W5 —1E 2
Octavia Rd. Iswth —7A 2
Odard Rd. W Mol —1F 19
Ogden Ho. Felt —7D 6
Oil Mill La. W6 —2D 4
Old Barn Rd. Eps —6K 27
Old Bri. St. Hamp W —6E 14
Old Brompton Rd. SW5 &
SW7 —2K 5
Old Claygate La. Clay —3B 24
Old Deer Pk. Gdns. Rich
—7F 3
Old Dock Clo. Rich —3H 3
Old Farm Clo. Houn —1E 6
Old Farm Pas. Hamp —5H 13
Old Farm Rd. Hamp —3E 12
Oldfield Gdns. Asht —7E 26
Oldfield Ho. W4 —2B 4
(off Devonshire Rd.)
Oldfield Rd. SW19 —3H 17
Oldfield Rd. Hamp —5E 12
Oldfields Rd. Sutt —7J 23
Oldfields Trading Est. Sutt
—7K 23
Old Ho. Clo. SW19 —2H 17
Old Ho. Gdns. Twic —3D 8
Old Kingston Rd. Wor Pk
—7K 21
Old Lodge Pl. Twic —3D 8
Old Malden La. Wor Pk
—6B 22
Old Manor Dri. Iswth —3H 7
Old Manor Yd. SW5 —1K 5
Old Orchard. Sun —6B 12
Old Palace La. Rich —2D 8
Old Palace Ter. Rich —2E 8
Old Palace Yd. Rich —2D 8
Old School Clo. SW19
—6K 17
Old School Sq. Th Dit
—3A 20
Oliver Clo. W4 —3J 3
Oliver Rd. N Mald —6K 15
Olivette St. SW15 —7G 5
Olympia Way. W14 —1H 5
Ongar Rd. SW6 —3K 5
Onslow Av. Rich —2F 9
Onslow Clo. Th Dit —5K 19
Onslow Gdns. Th Dit —5K 19
Onslow Rd. N Mald —1D 22
Onslow Rd. Rich —2F 9
Onslow Way. Th Dit —5K 19
Orbain Rd. SW6 —4H 5
Orchard Av. N Mald —7B 16
Orchard Av. Th Dit —1A 20
Orchard Clo. SW20 —1F 23
Orchard Clo. Surb —5C 20
Orchard Clo. W on T —4A 18
Orchard Clo. W Ewe —3J 25
Orchard Ct. Twic —6J 7

o. Hamp —5E **12**
o. Sun —4A **12**
o. W on T —7A **18**
res. Sutt —7G **23**
Jns. SW13 —7C **4**
Jns. W4 —1B **4**
Jns. Hamp —4E **12**
a. Rich —4H **3**
a. W Mol —1G **19**
a. W on T —7A **18**
d. W4 —1A **4**
d. Chess —7F **21**
d. Hamp —4E **12**
d. Houn —2H **7**
d. Rich —3H **3**
er. Sun —4A **12**
ade App. Rd. W4
—4B **4**
ade, The. W4 —5B **4**
Cotts. SW18 —1K **11**
Cres. Twic —3H **7**
Pl. W4 —2A **4**
t Rd. Surb —3D **20**
e Rd. SW6 —4H **5**
ugh Rd. SW18
—4J **11**
ugh Way. Houn
—1B **6**
Gdns. SW15 —3F **11**
l. SW6 —4K **5**
l. Bren —4F **2**
g Sta. Rd. W4 —4B **4**
Av. N Mald —3C **22**
res. SW4 —3C **22**
Clo. Asht —7G **27**
Ct. Wor Pk —5D **22**
Cross Rd. SW6 —5J **5**
Bri. SW15 & SW6
—7H **5**
Bri. App. SW6 —7H **5**
Bri. Rd. SW15 & SW18
—1H **11**
Comn. SW15 —7F **5**
Exchange Shopping
Cen. SW15 —1G **11**
Heath. SW15 —4E **10**
Heath La. SW15
—3G **11**
High St. SW15
—1G **11**
Hill. SW15 —4G **11**
parts)
Pk. Av. SW15 —1D **10**
Pk. La. SW15 —1E **10**
k Rd. Sutt —7K **23**
. Surb —5H **21**
Rd. Rich —3G **9**
Rd. W4 —3H **3**

nt Rd. Rich —1E **8**
t, The. SW20 —5H **17**
t, The. Rich —1F **9**
La. Iswth —4A **2**
k Dri. Wor Pk —6F **23**
don St. SW6 —6K **5**
nne Dri. Clay —4A **24**
nne's Clo. Twic
—7J **7**
nne's Gdns. W4
—1B **4**
nne's Gro. W4
—1B **4**
aroline St. W6 —1F **5**
lizabeth Gdns. Mord
—1K **23**
lizabeth Rd. King T
—6G **15**
lizabeth Wlk. SW13
—5D **4**
Mary Av. Mord
—2G **23**
Av. Felt —1A **12**
ridge Pk. Iswth
—2K **7**

Queensbury Ho. Rich —2E **8**
Queen's Club Gdns. W14
—3H **5**
Queens Ct. Rich —3G **9**
Queen's Cres. Rich —2G **9**
Queen's Dri. Surb —4H **21**
Queen's Dri. Th Dit —3B **20**
Queensfield Ct. Sutt —7F **23**
Queens Ga. Gdns. SW15
—1E **10**
Queens Ho. Tedd —3A **14**
Queensland Av. SW19
—5K **17**
Queensmere Clo. SW19
—6G **11**
Queensmere Ct. SW13 —3C **4**
Queensmere Rd. SW19
—6G **11**
Queensmill Rd. SW6 —4G **5**
Queens Pl. Mord —1K **23**
Queen's Promenade. King T
—1E **20**
Queens Reach. E Mol —1K **19**
Queens Reach. King T
—6E **14**
Queens Ride. SW13 & SW15
—7D **4**
Queens Rise. Rich —3G **9**
Queen's Rd. SW14 —7A **4**
Queens Rd. SW19 —3J **17**
Queen's Rd. Felt —5A **6**
Queen's Rd. Hamp —1G **13**
Queens Rd. King T —4H **15**
Queens Rd. Mord —1K **23**
Queens Rd. N Mald —1C **22**
Queen's Rd. Rich —4G **9**
Queen's Rd. Tedd —3A **14**
Queens Rd. Th Dit —2A **20**
Queens Rd. Twic —5B **8**
Queens Ter. Iswth —1B **8**
Queens Way. Felt —1B **12**
Queensway. Sun —6A **12**
Queenswood Av. Hamp
—3G **13**
Quennell Clo. Asht —7G **27**
Quick Rd. W4 —2B **4**
Quill Clo. W4 —2B **4**
Quintin Av. SW20 —5J **17**
Quinton Rd. Th Dit —5B **20**

**R**aby Rd. N Mald —1A **22**
Racton Rd. SW6 —3K **5**
Radbourne Av. W5 —1D **2**
Radcliffe M. Hamp —2H **13**
Radcliffe Sq. SW15 —3G **11**
Radipole Rd. SW6 —5J **5**
Radley M. W8 —1K **5**
Radnor Gdns. Twic —6A **8**
Radnor Rd. Twic —5A **8**
Radnor Ter. W14 —1J **5**
Raeburn Av. Surb —5J **21**
Raeburn Clo. King T —4E **14**
Raglan Clo. Houn —2E **6**
Railshead Rd. Iswth —1C **8**
Railway App. Twic —4B **8**
Railway Cotts. Twic —3F **7**
Railway Pas. Tedd —3B **14**
Railway Rd. Tedd —1K **13**
Railway Side. SW13 —7C **4**
Railway Ter. SW13 —6F **5**
Rainville Rd. W6 —3F **5**
Raleigh Dri. Surb —5K **21**
Raleigh Rd. Rich —7G **3**
Raleigh Way. Felt —2B **12**
Ramillies Rd. W4 —1A **4**
Ram Pl. King T —6E **14**
Ram St. SW18 —2K **11**
Randle Rd. Rich —1D **14**
Randolph Clo. King T —2K **15**
Ranelagh Av. SW6 —7J **5**
Ranelagh Av. SW13 —6D **4**
Ranelagh Dri. Twic —2C **8**
Ranelagh Gdns. SW6 —7H **5**
Ranelagh Gdns. W4 —4K **3**
Ranelagh Gdns. W6 —1C **4**

Ranelagh Gdns. Mans. SW6
(off Ranelagh Gdns.) —7H **5**
Ranelagh Pl. N Mald —2B **22**
Ranfurly Rd. Sutt —6K **23**
Rannoch Rd. W6 —3F **5**
Ranyard Clo. Chess —7G **21**
Ravenna Rd. SW15 —2G **11**
Ravensbourne Rd. Twic
—3D **8**
Ravensbury Rd. SW18
—6K **11**
Ravenscar Rd. Surb —6G **21**
Ravenscourt Av. W6 —1D **4**
Ravenscourt Gdns. W6 —1D **4**
Ravenscourt Pk. W6 —1D **4**
Ravenscourt Pk. Mans. W6
—1E **4**
(off Paddenswick Rd.)
Ravenscourt Pl. W6 —1E **4**
Ravenscourt Rd. W6 —1E **4**
Ravenscourt Sq. W6 —1D **4**
Ravenscroft Rd. W4 —1K **3**
Ravensmede Way. W4 —1C **4**
Ravenswood Av. Surb
—6G **21**
Ravenswood Ct. King T
—3J **15**
Ravenswood Gdns. Iswth
—5A **2**
Rawchester Clo. SW18
—5J **11**
Rawsthorne Ct. Houn —1E **6**
Raybell Ct. Iswth —6B **2**
Rayleigh Av. Tedd —3K **13**
Rayleigh Ct. King T —6H **15**
Rayleigh Rd. SW19 —5J **17**
Raymond Av. W13 —1B **2**
Raymond Rd. SW19 —3H **17**
Raymond Way. Clay —3B **24**
Rayners Rd. SW15 —2H **11**
Raynes Pk. Bri. SW20 —6F **17**
Raynham Rd. W6 —1E **4**
Ray Rd. W Mol —2G **19**
Read Rd. Asht —6E **26**
Reapers Way. Iswth —2J **7**
Reckitt Rd. W4 —2B **4**
Rectory Clo. SW20 —7F **17**
Rectory Clo. Asht —7G **27**
Rectory Clo. Surb —5D **20**
Rectory Ct. Felt —1B **12**
Rectory Gro. Hamp —1E **12**
Rectory La. Asht —7G **27**
Rectory La. Surb —5C **20**
Rectory Orchard. SW19
—1H **17**
Rectory Rd. SW13 —6D **4**
Rectory Rd. Sutt —7K **23**
Redcliffe Clo. SW5 —2K **5**
Redclose Av. Mord —2K **23**
Redesdale Gdns. Iswth —4B **2**
Redfern Av. Houn —4F **7**
Redfield La. SW5 —1K **5**
Redfield M. SW5 —1K **5**
Redgate Ter. SW15 —3G **11**
Redgrave Rd. SW15 —7G **5**
Red Ho. La. W on T —6A **18**
Redlands. Tedd —3B **14**
Redlands Gdns. W Mol
—1E **18**
Red La. Clay —3B **24**
Redlees Clo. Iswth —1B **8**
Red Lion Rd. Surb —6G **21**
Red Lion Sq. SW18 —2K **11**
Redmore Rd. W6 —1E **4**
Redway Dri. Twic —4H **7**
Redwood Ct. Surb —4E **20**
Redwoods. SW15 —5D **10**
Redwood Wlk. Surb —5E **20**
Regency Ct. Hamp —2E **12**
Regency Ct. Tedd —3C **14**
Regency Gdns. W on T
—5B **18**
Regency M. Iswth —2C **7**
Regency Wlk. Rich —2F **9**
(off Grosvenor Av.)

Regent Rd. Surb —2G **21**
Regent St. W4 —2H **3**
Reigate Av. Sutt —5K **23**
Relko Ct. Eps —7K **25**
Rembrandt Way. W on T
—6A **18**
Renfrew Rd. King T —4J **15**
Renmans, The. Asht —5G **27**
Rennels Way. Iswth —6A **2**
Replingham Rd. SW18
—5J **11**
Reporton Rd. SW6 —4H **5**
Restormel Clo. Houn —2F **7**
Retreat Rd. Rich —2E **8**
Retreat, The. SW14 —7B **4**
Retreat, The. Surb —3G **21**
Retreat, The. Wor Pk —7E **22**
Reubens Ct. W4 —2J **3**
(off Chaseley Dri.)
Revell Rd. King T —6J **15**
Revelstoke Rd. SW18 —6J **11**
Reynolds Av. Chess —4F **25**
Reynolds Pl. Rich —3G **9**
Reynolds Rd. N Mald —4A **22**
Rhodesmoor Ho. Ct. Mord
—3K **23**
Rhodrons Av. Chess —2F **25**
Ricards Rd. SW19 —2J **17**
Richbell Clo. Asht —7E **26**
Rich La. SW5 —2K **5**
Richmond Av. SW20 —5H **17**
Richmond Bri. Twic & Rich
—3E **8**
Richmond Cotts. W14 —1H **5**
(off Hammersmith Rd.)
Richmond Gro. Surb —3G **21**
Richmond Hill. Rich —3F **9**
Richmond Hill Ct. Rich —3F **9**
Richmond Mans. Twic —3E **8**
Richmond. M. Tedd —2A **14**
Richmond Pk. Rd. SW14
—2K **9**
Richmond Pk. Rd. King T
—4F **15**
Richmond Rd. SW20 —5E **16**
Richmond Rd. Iswth —7B **2**
Richmond Rd. King T —2E **14**
Richmond Rd. Twic —4C **8**
Rickards Clo. Surb —5F **21**
Rickett St. SW6 —3K **5**
Ride, The. Bren —1D **2**
Ridge Rd. Sutt —5H **23**
Ridge, The. Surb —2H **21**
Ridge, The. Eps —7K **27**
Ridge, The. Twic —4J **7**
Ridgeway. Eps —1K **27**
Ridgway. SW19 —4F **17**
Ridgway Gdns. SW19 —4G **17**
Ridgway Pl. SW19 —3H **17**
Ridings, The. Asht —6E **26**
Ridings, The. Surb —2H **21**
Ridley Av. W13 —1C **2**
Ridley Rd. SW19 —4K **17**
Rigault Rd. SW6 —6H **5**
Rigford Rd. SW18 —2J **
Ringmer Av. SW6 —5H **5**
Ringmore Rd. W on T —7B **18**
Ring Rd. SW6 —3K **5**
Ringwood Gdns. SW15
—5D **10**
Ringwood Way. Hamp
—1F **13**
Ripley Gdns. SW14 —7A **4**
Ripley Rd. Hamp —4F **13**
Ripon Gdns. Chess —5H **25**
Risborough Dri. Wor Pk
—4D **22**
River Av. Th Dit —4B **20**
River Bank. E Mol —7K **13**
River Bank. Th Dit —4A **20**
River Bank. W Mol —7F **13**
Riverbank Way. Bren —3D **2**
River Brent Bus. W. W7
—1A **2**

Rivercourt Rd. W6 —1E **4**
Riverdale Gdns. Twic —3D **8**
Riverdale Rd. Felt —1D **12**
Riverdale Rd. Twic —3D **8**
River Gdns. Felt —2A **6**
River Gdns. Bus. Cen. Houn
—1A **6**
Riverhill. Wor Pk —6A **22**
River La. Rich —5E **8**
Rivermead Clo. Tedd —2C **14**
Rivermead Ct. SW6 —7J **5**
River Meads Av. Twic —7F **7**
Rivernook Clo. W on T
—2B **18**
River Reach. Tedd —2D **14**
Riversdale Rd. Th Dit —2B **20**
Riverside. Rich —2E **8**
Riverside. Sun —6C **12**
Riverside. Twic —5C **8**
Riverside Av. E Mol —2J **19**
Riverside Av. Rich —5F **3**
Riverside Bus. Cen. SW18
—5K **11**
Riverside Bus. Cen. Twic
—1C **8**
Riverside Clo. King T —1E **20**
Riverside Ct. Iswth —6A **2**
(off Woodlands Rd.)
Riverside Dri. W4 —4A **4**
Riverside Dri. Rich —6C **8**
Riverside Gdns. W6 —2E **4**
Riverside Wlk. SW6 —7H **5**
Riverside Wlk. Iswth —7A **2**
Riverside Wlk. King T —7E **14**
River Ter. W6 —2F **5**
Riverview Gdns. SW13 —3E **4**
River View Gdns. Twic —6A **8**
Riverview Gro. W4 —3J **3**
Riverview Rd. W4 —4J **3**
River Vw. Eps —1K **25**
River Wlk. W6 —4F **5**
River Wlk. W on T —3A **18**
River Way. Twic —6G **7**
Robert Owen Ho. SW6 —5G **5**
(off Fulham Pal. Rd.)
Robin Clo. Hamp —2D **12**
Robin Gro. Bren —3D **2**
Robin Hood La. SW15
—1B **16**
SW15 —2D **16**
Robin Hood Way. SW19 &
SW20 —7B **10**
Rock Av. SW14 —7A **4**
Rockingham Clo. SW15
—1C **10**
Rockland Rd. SW15 —1H **11**
Rocks La. SW13 —5D **4**
Rocque Ho. SW6 —4J **5**
(off Estcourt Rd.)
Rodney Clo. N Mald —2B **22**
Rodney Clo. W on T —5B **18**
Rodney Grn. W on T —6B **18**
Rodney Rd. N Mald —2B **22**
Rodney Rd. Twic —3F **7**
Rodway Rd. SW15 —4D **10**
Roebuck Clo. Felt —1A **12**
Roebuck Rd. Chess —2H **25**
Roedean Cres. SW15 —3B **10**
Roehampton Clo. SW15
—1D **10**
Roehampton Gas. SW15
—3B **10**
Roehampton High St. SW15
—4D **10**
Roehampton La. SW15
—1D **10**
Roehampton Vale. SW15
—7C **10**
Rokeby Pl. SW20 —7E **16**
Roland Way. Wor Pk —6C **22**
Rollesby Rd. Chess —3H **25**
Rollit Cres. Houn —5F **7**
Roman Clo. Felt —2B **6**

Roman Rd. W4 —1C **4**
Romany Gdns. Sutt —4K **23**
Roma Read Clo. SW15
　　　　　　　　—4E **10**
Romily Ct. SW6 —6H **5**
Romney Clo. Chess —1F **25**
Romney Rd. N Mald —3A **22**
Romulus Ct. Bren —4E **2**
Ronelean Rd. Surb —7G **21**
Rookeries Clo. Felt —7B **6**
Rookery Hill. Asht —7H **27**
Rookwood Av. N Mald
　　　　　　　　—1D **22**
Rope Wlk. Sun —7B **12**
Rosaline Rd. SW6 —4H **5**
Rosaville Rd. SW6 —4J **5**
Rosebank. Eps —3K **27**
Roseberry Av. N Mald
　　　　　　　　—6C **16**
Rosebery Clo. Mord —3G **23**
Rosebery Rd. Houn —2H **7**
Rosebery Rd. King T —6J **15**
Rosebery Sq. King T —6J **15**
Rosebine Av. Twic —4J **7**
Rosecroft Gdns. Twic —5J **7**
Rose & Crown Pas. Iswth
　　　　　　　　—5B **2**
Rosedale. Asht —7D **26**
Rosedale Rd. Rich —1F **9**
*Rosedale Ter. W6 —1E **4***
　*(off Dalling Rd.)*
Rosedene Av. Mord —2C **23**
Rosedew Rd. W6 —3G **5**
Rose End. Wor Pk —5G **23**
Roseheath Rd. Houn —2E **6**
Rosehill. Clay —3B **24**
Rosehill. Hamp —5F **13**
Roseleigh Clo. Twic —3E **8**
Rosemary Av. W Mol —7F **13**
Rosemary Gdns. SW14
　　　　　　　　—7K **3**
Rosemary Gdns. Chess
　　　　　　　　—1F **25**
Rosemary La. SW14 —7K **3**
Rosemont Rd. N Mald
　　　　　　　　—7K **15**
Rosemont Rd. Rich —3F **9**
Roseville Av. Houn —2F **7**
Rosevine Rd. SW20 —5F **17**
Rose Wlk. Surb —2J **21**
Roskell Rd. SW15 —7G **5**
Rossdale Rd. SW15 —1F **11**
Rossindel Rd. Houn —2F **7**
Rosslyn Av. SW13 —7B **4**
Rosslyn Av. Felt —3A **6**
Rosslyn Rd. Twic —3D **8**
Ross Rd. Twic —5G **7**
Rostrevor M. SW6 —5J **5**
Rostrevor Rd. SW6 —5J **5**
Rostrevor Rd. SW19 —2K **17**
Rothbury Gdns. Iswth —4B **2**
Rotherwood Clo. SW20
　　　　　　　　—5H **17**
Rotherwood Rd. SW15 —7G **5**
Rothesay Av. SW20 —6H **17**
Rothesay Av. Rich —1J **9**
Rothschild Rd. W4 —1K **3**
Rougemont Av. Mord —3K **23**
Roundacre. SW19 —6G **11**
Roundway, The. Clay —3A **24**
Rowallan Rd. SW6 —4H **5**
Rowan Clo. N Mald —6B **16**
Rowan Rd. W6 —1G **5**
Rowan Rd. Bren —4C **2**
*Rowan Ter. W6 —1G **5***
　*(off Rowan Rd.)*
Rowberry Clo. SW6 —4F **5**
Rowden Rd. Eps —1J **25**
Rowhurst Av. Lea —6A **26**
Rowlls Rd. King T —7G **15**
Rowntree Rd. Twic —5K **7**
Roxborough Av. Iswth —4A **2**
Roxby Pl. SW6 —3K **5**
Royal Av. Wor Pk —6B **22**
Royal Clo. Wor Pk —6B **22**
Royal Gdns. W7 —1B **2**

Royal Orchard Clo. SW18
　　　　　　　　—4H **11**
Royal Pde. SW6 —4H **5**
Royal Pde. Rich —5H **3**
Royal Rd. Tedd —2J **13**
Roydon Ct. W on T —7A **18**
Roy Gro. Hamp —3G **13**
Roymount Ct. Twic —7K **7**
Royston Clo. W on T —5A **18**
Royston Ct. Rich —5G **3**
Royston Rd. Rich —2F **9**
Roystons, The. Surb —2J **21**
Rugby Rd. Twic —2K **7**
Rumsey Clo. Hamp —3E **12**
Running Horse Yd. Bren
　　　　　　　　—3F **3**
Runnymede Clo. Twic —3G **7**
Runnymede Ct. SW15
　　　　　　　　—5D **10**
Runnymede Gdns. Twic
　　　　　　　　—3G **7**
Runnymede Rd. Twic —3G **7**
Rupert Rd. W4 —1B **4**
Rushbury Ct. Hamp —5F **13**
Rushett Clo. Th Dit —5C **20**
Rushett La. Chess & Eps
　　　　　　　　—7D **24**
Rushett Rd. Th Dit —4C **20**
Rushey Clo. N Mald —1A **22**
Rushmead. Rich —7C **8**
Rushmere Ct. Wor Pk —6D **22**
Rushmere Pl. SW19 —2G **17**
Rushmon Gdns. W on T
　　　　　　　　—6A **18**
Rusholme Rd. SW15 —3G **11**
Ruskin Av. Rich —4H **3**
Ruskin Dri. Wor Pk —6E **22**
Ruskin Rd. Iswth —7A **2**
Russell Gdns. Rich —6D **8**
Russell Kerr Clo. W4 —4K **3**
Russell Rd. SW19 —4K **17**
Russell Rd. W14 —1H **5**
Russell Rd. Twic —3A **8**
Russell Wlk. Rich —3G **9**
Russell Yd. SW15 —1H **11**
Russet Clo. W on T —7D **18**
Rusthall Av. W4 —1A **4**
Rustington Wlk. Mord —4J **23**
Ruston Av. Surb —4J **21**
Ruthen Clo. Eps —3J **27**
Rutland Clo. SW14 —7J **3**
Rutland Clo. Chess —3G **25**
Rutland Dri. Mord —3J **23**
Rutland Dri. Rich —5F **9**
Rutland Gro. W6 —2E **4**
Rutland Rd. Twic —6J **7**
Rutlish Rd. SW19 —5K **17**
Ruvigny Gdns. SW15 —7G **5**
Ruxley Clo. Eps —2J **25**
Ruxley Ct. Wor Pk —2K **25**
Ruxley Cres. Clay —3C **24**
Ruxley La. Eps —3J **25**
Ruxley M. Eps —2J **25**
Ruxley Ridge. Clay —4B **24**
Rydal Gdns. SW15 —2B **16**
Rydal Gdns. Houn —3G **7**
Rydens Av. W on T —6A **18**
Rydens Clo. W on T —6B **18**
Rydens Gro. W on T —7C **18**
Rydens Pk. W on T —6C **18**
Rydens Rd. W on T —7A **18**
Ryde Pl. Twic —3E **8**
Ryebridge Clo. Lea —7B **26**
Ryebrook Rd. Lea —7B **26**
Ryecroft Av. Twic —4G **7**
Ryecroft St. SW6 —5K **5**
Ryefield Path. SW15 —5D **10**
Ryelands Ct. Lea —7B **26**
Rye Wlk. SW15 —2G **11**
Ryfold Rd. SW19 —7K **11**
Rylston Rd. SW6 —3J **5**
Rythe Ct. Th Dit —4B **20**

**S**adlers Ride. W Mol —7G **13**

Saffron Way. Surb —5E **20**
St Agatha's Dri. King T
　　　　　　　　—3G **15**
St Alban's Av. W4 —1A **4**
St Albans Av. Felt —2C **12**
St Alban's Gdns. Tedd
　　　　　　　　—2B **14**
St Alban's Rd. King T —3F **15**
St Alban's Ter. W6 —3H **5**
*St Andrews Mans. W14*
　*(off St Andrews Rd.)* —3H **5**
St Andrew's Rd. W14 —3H **5**
St Andrew's Rd. Surb —3E **20**
St Andrew's Sq. Surb —3E **20**
St Anne's Pas. SW13 —7B **4**
St Ann's Rd. SW13 —6C **4**
St Aubyn's Av. SW19 —2J **17**
St Aubyn's Av. Houn —2F **7**
St Catherine's Ct. W4 —1B **4**
St Chads Clo. Surb —4D **20**
St Clair Dri. Wor Pk —7E **22**
St Clare Bus. Pk. Hamp
　　　　　　　　—3H **13**
*St Clements Mans. SW6*
　*(off Lillie Rd.)* —3G **5**
St Dionis Rd. SW6 —6J **5**
St Dunstan's Hill. Sutt —7J **23**
St Dunstan's Rd. W6 —2G **5**
St Edmund's La. Twic —4G **7**
St George's Ct. SW15 —1J **11**
St George's Gdns. Surb
　　　　　　　　—6J **21**
St George's Pl. Twic —5B **8**
St George's Rd. SW19
　　　　　　　　—3J **17**
St George's Rd. Felt —1C **12**
St George's Rd. King T
　　　　　　　　—4H **15**
St Georges Rd. Rich —7G **3**
St George's Rd. Twic —2C **8**
St George's Sq. N Mald
　　　　　　　　—7B **16**
St Helens. Th Dit —4A **20**
St Helier's Av. Houn —2F **7**
St Hilda's Rd. SW13 —3E **4**
St James Clo. N Mald —2C **22**
St James Ct. Asht —6E **26**
St James' Rd. King T —6E **14**
St James's Av. Hamp —2H **13**
St James's Cotts. Rich —2E **8**
St James's Rd. Hamp
　　　　　　　　—2G **13**
St James's Rd. Surb —3E **20**
St James St. W6 —2F **5**
St John's Av. SW15 —2G **11**
St John's Clo. SW6 —4K **5**
*St John's Clo. W6 —1E **4***
　*(off Glenthorne Rd.)*
St John's Ct. Iswth —6A **2**
St John's Dri. W on T
　　　　　　　　—5B **18**
St John's Gro. SW13 —6C **4**
St John's Gro. Rich —1F **9**
St John's Pas. SW19 —3H **17**
St John's Rd. SW19 —4H **17**
St John's Rd. E Mol —1J **19**
St John's Rd. Felt —1D **12**
St John's Rd. Iswth —6A **2**
St John's Rd. King T —6D **14**
St John's Rd. N Mald —7K **15**
St John's Rd. Rich —1F **9**
St John's Rd. Sutt —6K **23**
St Lawrence Bus. Cen. Twic
　　　　　　　　—6A **6**
St Leonard's Rd. SW14
　　　　　　　　—7J **3**
St Leonard's Rd. Clay
　　　　　　　　—3A **24**
St Leonard's Rd. Surb
　　　　　　　　—2E **20**
St Leonard's Rd. Th Dit
　　　　　　　　—3B **20**
St Leonards Sq. Surb —2E **20**
St Luke's Pas. King T —5G **15**
St Margaret's Av. Sutt
　　　　　　　　—7H **23**

St Margarets Bus. Cen. Twic
　　　　　　　　—3C **8**
St Margaret's Cres. SW15
　　　　　　　　—2E **10**
St Margaret's Dri. Twic
　　　　　　　　—2C **8**
St Margaret's Gro. Twic
　　　　　　　　—3B **8**
St Margarets Rd. Iswth & Twic
　　　　　　　　—1C **8**
St Mark's Hill. Surb —3F **21**
St Mark's Pl. SW19 —3J **17**
St Mark's Rd. Tedd —4C **14**
St Martin's Dri. W on T
　　　　　　　　—7B **18**
*St Mary Abbot's Ct. W14*
　*(off Warwick Gdns.)* —1J **5**
St Mary Abbot's Pl. W8
　　　　　　　　—1J **5**
St Mary Abbot's Ter. W14
　　　　　　　　—1J **5**
St Mary's. Tedd —3A **14**
St Mary's Clo. Chess —4G **25**
St Mary's Gro. SW13 —7E **4**
St Mary's Gro. Rich —1G **9**
St Mary's La. W8 —1K **5**
St Marys M. Rich —6D **8**
St Mary's Pl. W8 —1K **5**
St Mary's Rd. SW19 —2H **17**
St Mary's Rd. Dit H —4D **20**
St Mary's Rd. E Mol —2J **19**
St Mary's Rd. Surb —3E **20**
St Mary's Rd. Wor Pk
　　　　　　　　—6B **22**
St Matthew's Av. Surb
　　　　　　　　—5F **21**
St Maur Rd. SW6 —5J **5**
St Michael's Clo. W on T
　　　　　　　　—6B **18**
St Michael's Clo. Wor Pk
　　　　　　　　—6C **22**
St Nicholas Rd. Th Dit
　　　　　　　　—3A **20**
St Olaf's Rd. SW6 —4H **5**
St Paul's Clo. Chess —1E **24**
St Paul's Rd. Bren —3E **2**
St Paul's Rd. Rich —7G **3**
*St Paul's Studios. W14*
　*(off Talgarth Rd.)* —2H **5**
St Paul's Wlk. King T —4H **15**
St Peters Ct. W Mol —1F **19**
St Peter's Gro. W6 —1D **4**
St Peter's Rd. W6 —2D **4**
St Peter's Rd. King T —6H **15**
St Peter's Rd. Twic —2C **8**
St Peter's Rd. W Mol —1F **19**
St Peter's Sq. W6 —1C **4**
St Peter's Ter. SW6 —4J **5**
St Peter's Vs. W6 —1D **4**
St Philip's Av. Wor Pk
　　　　　　　　—6E **22**
St Phillips Rd. Surb —3E **20**
St Simon's Av. SW15 —2F **11**
St Stephen's Av. Asht —5F **27**
St Stephen's Gdns. SW15
　　　　　　　　—2J **11**
St Stephen's Gdns. Twic
　　　　　　　　—3D **8**
St Stephen's Pas. Twic
　　　　　　　　—3D **8**
St Stephen's Rd. Houn —3F **7**
St Thomas Clo. Surb —5G **21**
St Thomas Rd. W4 —3K **3**
St Thomas's Way. SW6
　　　　　　　　—4J **5**
St Vincent Rd. Twic —3H **7**
St Vincent Rd. W on T
　　　　　　　　—7A **18**
St Winifred's Rd. Tedd
　　　　　　　　—3C **14**
Salcombe Dri. Mord —5G **23**
Salisbury Clo. Wor Pk
　　　　　　　　—7C **22**
Salisbury Gdns. SW19
　　　　　　　　—4H **17**

Salisbury M. SW6 —4
*Salisbury Pas. SW6—*
　*(off Dawes Rd.)*
Salisbury Rd. SW19 —
Salisbury Rd. Felt —
Salisbury Rd. Houn —
Salisbury Rd. N Mald
Salisbury Rd. Rich —
Salisbury Rd. Wor Pk
Salix Clo. Sun —4A **1**
Salliesfield. Twic —3
Salmons Rd. Chess —
Salvin Rd. SW15 —7
Samels Ct. W6 —2D **4**
*Samuel Lewis Trust D*
　　　　　　*SW6*
　*(off Vanston Pl.)*
*Samuel Lewis Trust D*
　*(off Lisgar Ter.) W14*
Sanctuary, The. Mord
Sandal Rd. N Mald —
Sandalwood Rd. Felt —
Sandbourne Av. SW19
Sanders Clo. Hamp —
Sandes Pl. Lea —7B **2**
Sandhurst Av. Surb —
Sandiford Rd. Sutt —
Sandon Clo. Esh —4J
Sandown Ga. Esh —
Sandown Ind. Pk. Esh
Sandown Rd. Esh —7
Sandpits Rd. Rich —6
Sandra Clo. Houn —2
Sandringham Av. SW2
Sandringham Rd. Wor
Sandycombe Rd. Felt
Sandycombe Rd. Rich
Sandycoombe Rd. Twic
Sandy La. Rich —6D
Sandy La. Tedd & King
Sandy La. W on T —
Sanger Av. Chess —2
Santos Rd. SW18 —2
*Sarjant Path. SW19 —*
　*(off Blincoe Clo.)*
Savile Clo. N Mald —1
Saville Rd. Twic —5A
Savill Gdns. SW20 —
Savona Clo. SW19 —
Sawkins Clo. SW19 —
Sawyers Hill. Rich —4
Saxon Av. Felt —6D **6**
Saxonbury Av. Sun —
Saxonbury Gdns. Surb
Saxon Clo. Surb —3E
Saxon Ho. Felt —6E **6**
Saxon Rd. W on T —
Sayer's Wlk. Rich —4
Scarsdale Vs. W8 —1
Scarth Rd. SW13 —7
School All. Twic —5B
School La. King T —4
School La. Surb —5H
School Pas. King T —
School Rd. E Mol —1
School Rd. Hamp —3
School Rd. King T —1
School Rd. Av. Hamp
Schubert Rd. SW15 —
Scott Clo. Eps —2K **2**
Scott Farm Clo. Th Dit
Scotts Dri. Hamp —4
Scotts Farm Rd. Eps —
Seaforth Av. N Mald —
Seaforth Gdns. Eps —

Rd. SW6 —3K **5**
 Clo. SW15 —5E **10**
lo. Twic —3J **7**
d. Twic —3H **7**
Av. W on T —3A **18**
Clo. W Mol —1H **19**
Cross Rd. Twic
—6K **7**
Rd. SW18 —3J **11**
mbe Rd. SW6 —3K **5**
Wells La. Surb
—3D **20**
t. SW15 —7F **5**
SW5 —1K **5**
omwell Rd.)
Ter. Felt —7F **7**
Rd. N Mald —6B **16**
e Av. Surb —6G **21**
. Chess —4F **25**
Clo. SW19 —5G **11**
d. Twic —6H **7**
Clo. Surb —2F **21**
Rd. Chess —1E **24**
Clo. Houn —1D **6**
Rd. N Mald —2A **22**
e Rd. Sutt —7G **23**
Ind. Est. SW18
—3K **11**
Houses. W on T
enue, The.) —6C **22**
Ct. Bren —4E **2**
on Rd. SW6 —6K **5**
ri. Esh —6B **20**
ri. W on T —6C **18**
Av. Mord —4G **23**
Clo. E Mol —2H **19**
Gdns. Felt —1B **12**
Gdns. Surb —2G **21**
Gdns. Twic —4C **8**
Rd. SW18 —4J **11**
Rd. SW19 —7G **11**
Rd. W4 —1K **3**
Rd. E Mol —2H **19**
Rd. Hamp —2H **13**
Rd. King T —5E **14**
gate La. Tedd —1K **13**
Clo. Wor Pk —6C **22**
ay. Tedd —4B **14**
ury Av. Felt —3A **6**
ury Rd. Rich —7F **3**
ury Way. Twic —7J **7**
eare Way. Felt
—1B **12**
Dri. Mord —2H **23**
Way. W on T
—7B **18**
e Rd. SW14 —7J **3**
Vs. Surb —3G **21**
t. SW18 —5K **11**
Clo. Eps —2K **27**
Clo. Surb —6C **8**
Rd. W4 —2A **4**
i. W on T —4B **18**
d Ct. SW15 —4D **10**
d Rd. Eps —3K **25**
Path. King T —5D **14**
gh St. Hampton Wick)
Dri. Cars —4K **23**
omn. Dri. Rich
—1H **9**
t. Rd. Rich —1H **9**
le Rd. Rich —1G **9**
a. Gdns. SW14
—1K **9**
a. SW14 —2K **9**
k. Rich —1F **9**
d. Rich —2F **9**
ood. SW14 —2K **9**
ouse Way. N Mald
—5A **22**
lk. M. SW19
—3G **17**
Rd. SW19 —5K **17**

Shepherd's Bush Rd. W6
—1F **5**
Sheppard Clo. King T —1F **21**
Sheraton Dri. Eps —2K **27**
Sherborne Rd. Chess —2F **25**
Sherborne Rd. Sutt —6K **23**
Shere Clo. Chess —2E **24**
Sherfield Gdns. SW15
—3C **10**
Sheridan Ct. Houn —2D **6**
Sheridan Pl. SW13 —7C **4**
Sheridan Pl. Hamp —5G **13**
Sheridan Rd. SW19 —5J **17**
Sheridan Rd. Rich —7D **8**
Sheringham Av. Twic —5E **6**
Sherland Rd. Twic —5A **8**
Sherwood Clo. SW13 —7E **4**
Sherwood Rd. SW19 —4J **17**
Sherwood Rd. Hamp —2H **13**
Shield Dri. Bren —3B **2**
Shingle End. Bren —4D **2**
Ship All. W4 —3H **3**
Ship La. SW14 —7K **3**
Shires Clo. Asht —7E **26**
Shires, The. Ham —1F **15**
Shirley Clo. Houn —2H **7**
Shirley Dri. Houn —2H **7**
Shore Clo. Hamp —3D **12**
Shore Gro. Felt —6F **7**
Shorrold's Rd. SW6 —4J **5**
Shortlands. W6 —1G **5**
Shortlands Rd. King T
—4G **15**
Short Rd. W4 —3B **4**
Short Way. Twic —4H **7**
Shotfield Av. SW14 —1B **10**
Shottendane Rd. SW6 —5K **5**
Shrewsbury Av. SW14
—1A **10**
Shrewsbury Clo. Surb
—6F **21**
Shrewsbury Wlk. Iswth
—7B **2**
Shrubland Gro. Wor Pk
—7F **23**
Sidbury St. SW6 —5H **5**
Sidney Gdns. Bren —3E **2**
Sidney Rd. Twic —3B **8**
Sidney Rd. W on T —4A **18**
Silver Cres. W4 —1J **3**
Silverdale Dri. Sun —6A **12**
Silverglade Bus. Pk. Chess
—1D **26**
Silverhall St. Iswth —7B **2**
Silverton Rd. W6 —3G **5**
Silver Tree Clo. W on T
—7A **18**
Simpson Rd. Houn —3E **6**
Simpson Rd. Rich —1D **14**
Simrose Ct. SW18 —2K **11**
Sinclair Rd. W14 —1H **5**
Sion Ct. Twic —5C **8**
Sion Rd. Twic —5C **8**
Sir Cyril Black Way. SW19
—4K **17**
Sir Oswald Stoll Foundation,
The. SW6 —4K **5**
(off Fulham Rd.)
Sir William Powell's
Almshouses. SW6 —6H **5**
Sispara Gdns. SW18 —3J **11**
Sixth Cross Rd. Twic —7H **7**
Skeena Hill. SW18 —4H **11**
Skelgill Rd. SW15 —1J **11**
Skelwith Rd. W6 —3F **5**
Skerne Rd. King T —5E **14**
Skinners La. Asht —7E **26**
Smallberry Av. Iswth —6A **2**
Smeaton Rd. SW18 —4K **11**
Smith Hill. Bren —3F **3**
Smith St. Surb —3G **21**
Smithwood Clo. SW19
—5H **11**
Smoothfield. Houn —1F **7**
Snowdrop Clo. Hamp —3F **12**

Snowy Fielder Waye. Iswth
—6C **2**
Soames Wlk. N Mald —5B **16**
Solna Av. SW15 —2F **11**
Somer Ct. SW6 —3K **5**
(off Anselm Rd.)
Somerset Av. SW20 —6E **16**
Somerset Av. Chess —1E **24**
Somerset Clo. N Mald
—3B **22**
Somerset Gdns. Tedd —2K **13**
Somerset Lodge. Bren —3E **2**
Somerset Rd. SW19 —7G **11**
Somerset Rd. Bren —3D **2**
Somerset Rd. King T —6G **15**
Somerset Rd. Tedd —2K **13**
Somerton Av. Rich —7J **3**
Sonning Gdns. Hamp —3D **12**
Sontan Ct. Twic —5J **7**
Sopwith Av. Chess —2F **25**
Sopwith Clo. King T —2G **15**
Sopwith Way. King T —5F **15**
Sorrento Rd. Sutt —7K **23**
Souldern Rd. W14 —1G **5**
South Av. Rich —6H **3**
South Bank. Surb —3F **21**
Southbank. Th Dit —4C **20**
S. Bank Ter. Surb —3F **21**
Southborough Clo. Surb
—5E **20**
Southborough Rd. Surb
—5F **21**
South Clo. Mord —3K **23**
South Clo. Twic —7F **7**
Southcombe St. W14 —1H **5**
Southcote Av. Surb —4J **21**
Southdean Gdns. SW19
—6J **11**
Southdown Av. W7 —1B **2**
Southdown Dri. SW20
—4G **17**
Southdown Rd. SW20
—5G **17**
Southdown Rd. W on T
—7D **18**
S. Edwardes Sq. W8 —1J **5**
Southerton Rd. W6 —1F **5**
Southey Rd. SW19 —4K **17**
Southfield Gdns. Twic
—1A **14**
Southfields. E Mol —3K **19**
Southfields Ct. Sutt —6K **23**
Southfields Pas. SW18
—3K **11**
Southfields Rd. SW18
—3K **11**
Southland Way. Houn —2J **7**
South La. King T —7E **14**
South La. N Mald —1A **22**
South La. W. N Mald —1A **22**
S. Lodge. Twic —4H **7**
Southly Clo. Sutt —7K **23**
Southmead Dri. SW19
—5H **11**
Southmont Rd. Esh —6K **19**
South Pde. W4 —1A **4**
South Pk. Gro. N Mald
—1K **21**
S. Park M. SW6 —7K **5**
Sth. Pk. Rd. SW19 —3K **17**
South Pl. Surb —4G **21**
Southridge Pl. SW20 —4G **17**
South Rd. W5 —1E **2**
South Rd. Felt —2C **12**
South Rd. Hamp —3D **12**
South Rd. Twic —7J **7**
Southsea Rd. King T —1F **21**
South Side. W6 —1C **4**
Southside Comn. SW19
—3F **17**
South St. Eps —2K **27**
South St. Iswth —7B **2**
South Ter. Surb —3F **21**
S. View Rd. Asht —7E **26**
Southville Rd. Th Dit —4C **20**

Southway. SW20 —1F **23**
S. Western Rd. Twic —3B **8**
Southwood Av. King T
—5K **15**
Southwood Clo. Wor Pk
—5G **23**
Southwood Dri. Surb —4K **21**
Southwood Gdns. Esh
—7B **20**
S. Worple Av. SW14 —7B **4**
S. Worple Way. SW14 —7A **4**
Sovereign Ct. Houn —1F **7**
Sovereign Ct. W Mol —1E **18**
Space Waye. Felt —2A **6**
Spa Dri. Eps —3H **27**
Sparks Clo. Hamp —3D **12**
Sparrow Clo. Hamp —3D **12**
Sparrow Farm Dri. Felt —4B **6**
Spear M. SW5 —1K **5**
Speer Rd. Th Dit —3A **20**
Speirs Clo. N Mald —3C **22**
Spencer Gdns. SW14 —2K **9**
Spencer Hill. SW19 —3H **17**
Spencer M. W6 —3H **5**
Spencer Pk. E Mol —2H **19**
Spencer Rd. SW20 —5E **16**
Spencer Rd. W4 —4K **3**
Spencer Rd. E Mol —1H **19**
Spencer Rd. Twic —7K **7**
Spencer Wlk. SW15 —1G **11**
Spicer Clo. W on T —3B **18**
Spinney Clo. N Mald —2B **22**
Spinney, The. SW13 —3E **4**
Spinney, The. Sun —5A **12**
Spray La. Twic —3K **7**
Spreighton Rd. W Mol
—1G **19**
Spring Cotts. Surb —2E **20**
Springfield Av. SW20 —7J **17**
Springfield Av. Hamp —3G **13**
Springfield Pl. N Mald
—1K **21**
Springfield Rd. SW19 —2J **17**
Springfield Rd. King T
—7F **15**
Springfield Rd. Tedd —2B **14**
Springfield Rd. Twic —5F **7**
Spring Gdns. W Mol —2G **19**
Spring Gro. W4 —2H **3**
Spring Gro. Hamp —5G **13**
Spring Gro. Rd. Rich —2G **9**
Spring Ter. Rich —2F **9**
Springvale Av. Bren —2F **3**
Spurfield. W Mol —7G **13**
Spur Rd. Felt —1A **6**
Spur Rd. Iswth —4B **2**
Square, The. W6 —2F **5**
Square, The. Rich —2E **8**
Squires Clo. SW19 —1K **17**
Squirrels Ct. Wor Pk —6C **22**
(off Avenue, The)
Squirrels Grn. Wor Pk
—6C **22**
Stable Yd. SW15 —7F **5**
Stafford Cripps Ho. SW6
(off Clem Attlee Ct.) —3J **5**
Stafford Pl. Rich —4G **9**
Stafford Rd. N Mald —7K **15**
Stag La. SW15 —7C **10**
Stags Way. Iswth —4A **2**
Staines Av. Sutt —6G **23**
Staines Rd. Felt & Houn
—3A **6**
Staines Rd. Twic —2D **14**
Staines Rd. E. Sun —4A **12**
Stamford Brook Av. W6
—1C **4**
Stamford Brook Gdns. W6
—1C **4**
Stamford Brook Mans. W6
(off Goldhawk Rd.) —1C **4**
Stamford Brook Rd. W6
—1C **4**
Stamford Ct. W6 —1D **4**
Stamford Grn. Rd. Eps
—2J **27**

Stamford Rd. W on T —7C **18**
Stanborough Clo. Hamp
—3E **12**
Stanbridge Rd. SW15 —7F **5**
Standard Rd. Houn —1D **6**
Standen Rd. SW18 —4J **11**
Standish Ho. W6 —1D **4**
(off St Peter's Gro.)
Standish Rd. W6 —1D **4**
Stanford Clo. Hamp —3E **12**
Stanier Clo. W14 —2J **5**
Stanley Av. N Mald —2D **22**
Stanley Gdns. Rd. Tedd
—2K **13**
Stanley Rd. SW14 —1J **9**
Stanley Rd. SW19 —3K **17**
Stanley Rd. Houn —1H **7**
Stanley Rd. Mord —1K **23**
Stanley Rd. Twic & Tedd
—1J **13**
Stanmore Gdns. Rich —7G **3**
Stanmore Rd. Rich —7G **3**
Stanton Av. Tedd —3K **13**
Stanton Clo. Eps —2J **25**
Stanton Clo. Wor Pk —5G **23**
Stanton Rd. SW13 —6C **4**
Stanton Rd. SW20 —5G **17**
Stanwick Rd. W14 —1J **5**
Stapleford Clo. SW19 —4H **11**
Stapleford Clo. King T
—6H **15**
Star & Garter Hill. Rich —5F **9**
Starling Wlk. Hamp —2D **12**
Star Rd. W14 —3J **5**
Staten Gdns. Twic —5A **8**
Station App. SW6 —7H **5**
Station App. Eps —2K **27**
Station App. Hamp —5F **13**
Station App. Hin W —7A **20**
Station App. King T —6H **15**
Station App. Rich —4K **3**
Station App. Sun —5A **12**
Station App. Wor Pk —5D **22**
Station App. Rd. W4 —4K **3**
Station Av. N Mald —7B **16**
Station Av. Rich —5H **3**
Station Av. W on T —7A **18**
Station Clo. Hamp —5G **13**
Station Est. Rd. Felt —5A **6**
Station Gdns. W4 —4K **3**
Station Pde. Felt —5A **6**
Station Pde. Rich —5H **3**
Station Rd. SW13 —6C **4**
Station Rd. Chess —2F **25**
Station Rd. Esh —6J **19**
Station Rd. Hamp —5F **13**
Station Rd. Hamp W —5E **14**
Station Rd. Houn —1G **7**
Station Rd. King T —5H **15**
Station Rd. N Mald —2E **22**
Station Rd. Tedd —2A **14**
Station Rd. Th Dit —4A **20**
Station Rd. Twic —5A **8**
Station Yd. Twic —4B **8**
Staunton Rd. King T —3F **15**
Staveley Gdns. W4 —5A **4**
Staveley Rd. W4 —3K **3**
Stayton Rd. Sutt —7K **23**
Steadfast Rd. King T —5E **14**
Steele Rd. Iswth —1B **8**
Steeple Clo. SW6 —6H **5**
Steeple Clo. SW19 —2H **17**
Stephenson Rd. Twic —4F **7**
Sterling Pl. W5 —1F **3**
Sterndale Rd. W14 —1G **5**
Sterry Dri. Eps —7B **22**
Sterry Dri. Th Dit —3K **19**
Steve Biko Way. Houn —1F **7**
Stevenage Rd. SW6 —4G **5**
Stevens Clo. Hamp —2D **12**
Stevens La. Clay —4B **24**
Stewart Clo. Hamp —3D **12**
Steyning Way. Houn —1B **6**
Stile Hall Gdns. W4 —2H **3**
Stile Hall Pde. W4 —2H **3**
Stile Path. Sun —7A **12**

Stillingfleet Rd. SW13 —3D **4**
Stirling Rd. Twic —5F **7**
Stirling Wlk. Surb —3J **21**
Stockhurst Clo. SW15 —6G **5**
Stokenchurch St. SW6 —5K **5**
Stoke Rd. King T —4K **15**
Stoke Rd. W on T —7B **18**
Stokesby Rd. Chess —3G **25**
Stompond La. W on T
—6A **18**
Stonecot Clo. Sutt —5H **23**
Stonecot Hill. Sutt —5H **23**
Stonehall Pl. W8 —1K **5**
Stonehill Clo. SW14 —2A **10**
Stonehill Rd. SW14 —2A **10**
Stone Hill Rd. W4 —2H **3**
Stoneleigh Av. Wor Pk
—7D **22**
Stone Pl. Wor Pk —6D **22**
Stoneydeep. Tedd —1B **14**
Stonny Croft. Asht —6G **27**
Stonor Rd. W14 —1J **5**
Stopford Clo. SW19 —4H **11**
Stormont Way. Chess —2D **24**
Stoughton Clo. SW15 —5D **10**
Stourhead Clo. SW19 —4G **11**
Stourhead Gdns. SW20
—7D **16**
Stourton Av. Felt —1E **12**
Strachan Pl. SW19 —3F **17**
Strafford Rd. Houn —1E **6**
Strafford Rd. Twic —4B **8**
Strand on the Grn. W4 —3H **3**
Strand School App. W4
—3H **3**
Stratford Av. W8 —1K **5**
Stratford Ct. N Mald —1A **22**
Stratford Gro. SW15 —1G **11**
Stratford Rd. W8 —1K **5**
Strathan Clo. SW18 —3J **11**
Strathearn Av. Twic —5G **7**
Strathearn Rd. SW19 —2K **17**
Strathmore Rd. SW19 —7K **11**
Strathmore Rd. Tedd —1K **13**
Strathville Rd. SW18 —6K **11**
Stratton Clo. SW19 —6K **17**
Stratton Clo. W on T —5B **18**
Stratton Rd. SW19 —6K **17**
Strawberry Hill. Twic —7A **8**
Strawberry Hill Clo. Twic
—7A **8**
Strawberry Hill Rd. Twic
—7A **8**
Strawberry Vale. Twic —7B **8**
Street, The. Asht —7G **27**
Stretton Rd. Rich —6D **8**
Strode Rd. SW6 —4H **5**
Stroud Cres. SW15 —7D **10**
Stroudes Clo. Wor Pk —4B **22**
Stroud Rd. SW19 —7K **11**
Stuart Av. W on T —5A **18**
Stuart Gro. Tedd —2K **13**
Stuart Rd. SW19 —7K **11**
Stuart Rd. Rich —6C **8**
Stubbs Ct. W4 —2J **3**
(off Chaseley Dri.)
Studdridge St. SW6 —6K **5**
Studland Rd. King T —3F **15**
Studland St. W6 —1E **4**
Sudbrook Gdns. Rich —7F **9**
Sudbrook La. Rich —5F **9**
Sudlow Rd. SW18 —2K **11**
Suffolk Rd. SW13 —4C **4**
Suffolk Rd. Wor Pk —6C **22**
Sugden Rd. Th Dit —5C **20**
Sulivan Ct. SW6 —6K **5**
Sulivan Enterprise Cen. SW6
—7K **5**
Sulivan Rd. SW6 —7K **5**
Sullivan Clo. W Mol —7G **13**
Summer Av. E Mol —2K **19**
Summerfield. Asht —7E **27**
Summerfield La. Surb —6E **20**
Summer Gdns. E Mol —2K **19**
Summer Rd. E Mol & Th Dit
—2K **19**

Summer Trees. Sun —5A **12**
Summerwood Rd. Iswth
—2A **8**
Summit Bus. Pk. Sun —4A **12**
Sun All. Rich —1F **9**
Sunbury Av. SW14 —1A **10**
Sunbury Ct. M. Sun —6C **12**
Sunbury Ct. Rd. Sun —6B **12**
Sunbury La. W on T —3A **18**
Sunbury Rd. Sutt —7H **23**
Sunbury Way. Felt —2B **12**
Sunna Gdns. Sun —6A **12**
Sunnindale Av. Felt —6D **6**
Sunningdale Clo. Surb
—6F **21**
Sunningdale Ct. Houn —3J **7**
(off Whitton Dene)
Sunningdale Rd. Sutt —7J **23**
Sunnybank. Eps —5K **27**
Sunnyhurst Clo. Sutt —7K **23**
Sunnymead Rd. SW15
—2E **10**
Sunnyside. SW19 —3H **17**
Sunnyside. W on T —2B **18**
Sunnyside Pas. SW19
—3H **17**
Sunnyside Rd. Tedd —1J **13**
Sunray Av. Surb —6J **21**
Sunrise Clo. Felt —7E **6**
Sun Rd. W14 —2J **5**
Surbiton Ct. Surb —3D **20**
Surbiton Cres. King T —1F **21**
Surbiton Hall Clo. King T
—1F **21**
Surbiton Hill Pk. Surb —2G **21**
Surbiton Hill Rd. Surb —2F **21**
Surbiton Pde. Surb —3F **21**
Surbiton Rd. King T —1E **20**
Surrey Cres. W4 —2H **3**
Sussex Av. Iswth —1K **7**
Sussex Clo. N Mald —1B **22**
Sussex Clo. Twic —3D **8**
Sussex Gdns. Chess —3E **24**
Sussex Pl. W6 —2F **5**
Sussex Pl. N Mald —1B **22**
Sussex Rd. N Mald —1B **22**
Sutherland Gdns. SW14
—7B **4**
Sutherland Gdns. Wor Pk
—5E **22**
Sutherland Gro. SW18
—3H **11**
Sutherland Gro. Tedd —2K **13**
Sutton Comn. Rd. Sutt
—4J **23**
Sutton Ct. W4 —3K **3**
Sutton Ct. Rd. W4 —4K **3**
Sutton La. N. W4 —2K **3**
Sutton La. S. W4 —3K **3**
Swallow Pk. Surb —7H **21**
Swan Clo. Felt —1D **12**
Swan Ct. Iswth —7C **2**
(off Swan St.)
Swan Pl. SW13 —6C **4**
Swan Rd. Felt —2D **12**
Swanscombe Rd. W4 —2B **4**
Swan St. Iswth —7C **2**
Swanton Gdns. SW19
—5G **11**
Sweet Briar La. Eps —3K **27**
Swift Rd. Felt —1C **12**
Swift St. SW6 —5J **5**
Swinburne Rd. SW15 —1D **10**
Swinfield Clo. Felt —7D **6**
Swyncombe Av. W5 —1C **2**
Sycamore Clo. Felt —7A **6**
Sycamore Ct. Houn —1D **6**
Sycamore Ct. N Mald —7B **16**
Sycamore Gro. N Mald
—7A **16**
Sycamore Rd. SW19 —3F **17**
Sycamore Way. Tedd —3D **14**
Sydney Rd. SW20 —6G **17**
Sydney Rd. Felt —5A **6**
Sydney Rd. Rich —1F **9**

Sydney Rd. Tedd —2A **14**
Sylvan Gdns. Surb —4E **20**
Sylvestrus Clo. King T
—5H **15**
Syon Ga. Way. Bren —4B **2**
Syon La. Iswth —3A **2**
Syon Pk. Gdns. Iswth —4A **2**

**T**abor Gro. SW19 —4H **17**
Tabor Rd. W6 —1E **4**
Tadworth Av. N Mald —2C **22**
Talbot Rd. Iswth —1B **8**
Talbot Rd. Twic —5K **7**
Talgarth Mans. W14 —2H **5**
(off Talgarth Rd.)
Talgarth Rd. W6 & W14
—2G **5**
Talma Gdns. Twic —3K **7**
Tamesis Gdns. Wor Pk
—6B **22**
Tamian Way. Houn —1B **6**
Tamworth St. SW6 —3K **5**
Tangier Rd. Rich —1H **9**
Tanglewood Way. Felt —7A **6**
Tangley Gro. SW15 —3C **10**
Tangley Pk. Rd. Hamp —2E **12**
Tankerton Rd. Surb —6G **21**
Tanners Clo. W on T —3A **18**
Tasso Rd. W6 —3H **5**
Tasso Yd. W6 —3H **5**
(off Tasso Rd.)
Taunton Av. SW20 —6E **16**
Taunton Clo. Sutt —5K **23**
Tawny Clo. Felt —7A **6**
Tayben Av. Twic —3K **7**
Taylor Av. Rich —6J **3**
Taylor Clo. Hamp —2H **13**
Taylor Rd. Asht —6E **26**
Tealing Dri. Eps —5K **27**
Teazlewood Pk. Lea —6B **26**
Tedder Clo. Chess —2D **24**
Teddington Pk. Tedd —2A **14**
Teddington Pk. Rd. Tedd
—1A **14**
Teesdale Av. Iswth —5B **2**
Teesdale Gdns. Iswth —5B **2**
Telegraph La. Clay —2A **24**
Telegraph Rd. SW15 —4E **10**
Telephone Pl. SW6 —3J **5**
Telford Dri. W on T —4B **18**
Telford Rd. Twic —4F **7**
Tellisford. Esh —7G **19**
Temple Clo. Eps —1K **27**
Templecombe Way. Mord
—2H **23**
Temple Rd. W4 —1K **3**
Temple Rd. W5 —1E **2**
Temple Rd. Eps —1K **27**
Temple Rd. Houn —1H **7**
Temple Rd. Rich —6G **3**
Temple Sheen. SW14 —2K **9**
Temple Sheen Rd. SW14
—1J **9**
Templeton Pl. SW5 —1K **5**
Tennis Ct. La. E Mol —7A **14**
Tennyson Av. N Mald —2E **22**
Tennyson Av. Twic —5A **8**
Terrace Gdns. SW13 —6C **4**
Terrace La. Rich —3F **9**
Terrace Rd. W on T —4A **18**
Terrace, The. SW13 —6B **4**
Thackeray Clo. SW19 —4G **17**
Thackeray Rd. SW14 —1H **5**
(off Blythe Rd.)
Thames Bank. SW14 —6K **3**
Thames Clo. Hamp —6G **13**
Thamesgate Clo. Rich
—1C **14**
Thameside. Tedd —4E **14**
Thameside. W Mol —7G **13**
Thameside Cen. Bren —3G **3**
Thames Lock. Sun —7A **12**
Thames Mead. W on T
—3A **18**

Thames Meadow. W Mol
—6F **13**
Thames Pl. SW15 —7G **5**
(in two parts)
Thames Rd. W4 —3H **3**
Thames Rd. Rich —3H **3**
Thames Side. King T —5E **14**
Thames St. Hamp —5G **13**
Thames St. King T —6E **14**
Thames St. Sun —1A **18**
Thamesview Houses. W on T
—3A **18**
Thames Village. W4 —5K **3**
Thatchers Way. Iswth —2J **7**
Thaxted Pl. SW20 —4G **17**
Thaxton Rd. W14 —3J **5**
Theatre Ct. Eps —2K **27**
Thelma Gro. Tedd —3B **14**
Theresa Rd. W6 —1D **4**
Thetford Rd. N Mald —3A **22**
Thetis Ter. Rich —3H **3**
Third Clo. W Mol —1H **19**
Third Cross Rd. Twic —6J **7**
Thistledene. Th Dit —3K **19**
Thomas Pl. W8 —1K **5**
Thompson Av. Rich —7H **3**
Thorkhill Gdns. Th Dit —5B **20**
Thorkhill Rd. Th Dit —5B **20**
Thorndon Gdns. Eps —7C **22**
Thorne Pas. SW13 —6B **4**
Thorne St. SW13 —7B **4**
Thorneycroft Clo. W on T
—3B **18**
Thorney Hedge Rd. W4 —1J **3**
Thornhill Av. Surb —6F **21**
Thornhill Ho. W4 —2B **4**
(off Wood St.)
Thornhill Rd. Surb —6F **21**
Thornton Av. W4 —1B **4**
Thornton Hill. SW19 —4H **17**
Thornton Rd. SW14 —1A **10**
Thornton Rd. SW19 —3G **17**
Thornton Rd. E. SW19
—3G **17**
Thornycroft Ho. W4 —2B **4**
(off Fraser St.)
Thorpe Rd. King T —4F **15**
Thrigby Rd. Chess —3G **25**
Thurleston Av. Mord —2H **23**
Thurnby Ct. Twic —7F **7**
Thursley Gdns. SW19
—6G **11**
Thurston Rd. SW20 —4E **16**
Tibbet's Clo. SW19 —5G **11**
Tibbet's Ride. SW15 —4G **11**
Tichmarsh. Eps —7K **25**
Tideswell Rd. SW15 —1H **5**
Tideway Clo. Rich —1C **14**
Tildesley Rd. SW15 —3F **11**
Tilford Gdns. SW19 —5G **11**
Tilton St. SW6 —3H **5**
Timbercroft. Eps —7B **22**
Timberhill. Asht —7F **27**
Timsbury Wlk. SW15 —5D **10**
Tinderbox All. SW14 —7A **4**
Tintern Clo. SW15 —2H **11**
Tiree Clo. Rich —5E **8**
Tithe Barn Clo. King T
—5G **15**
Tiverton Way. Chess —2E **24**
Tivoli Rd. Houn —1D **6**
Token Yd. SW15 —1H **11**
Toland Sq. SW15 —2D **10**
Tolson Rd. Iswth —7B **2**
Tolverne Rd. SW20 —5F **17**
Tolworth Clo. Surb —5J **21**
Tolworth Pk. Rd. Surb
—6G **21**
Tolworth Rise N. Surb —5J **21**
Tolworth Rise S. Surb —5J **21**
Tolworth Rd. Surb —6F **21**
Tolworth Tower. Surb —6J **21**
Tomlin Clo. Eps —7K **25**
Tomlin Ct. Eps —7K **25**
Tomlins All. Twic —5B **8**
Tomlinson Clo. W4 —2J **3**

Tom Williams Ho. SW
(off Clem Attlee Ct.)
Tonbridge Rd. W Mol
Tonfield Rd. Sutt —5
Tonstall Rd. Eps —6F
Topiary Sq. Rich —7F
Torrington Rd. Clay —
Torrington Way. Morc
Torwood Rd. SW15 —
Tournay Rd. SW6 —7
Tower Rise. Rich —7F
Tower Rd. Twic —7A
Towers Pl. Rich —2F
Tower Yd. Rich —2G
Towfield Ct. Felt —6E
Towfield Rd. Felt —6E
Town Hall Av. W4 —
Town Meadow. Bren
Town Meadow Rd. Bre
Townmead Rd. Rich —
Townshend Rd. Rich
Townshend Ter. Rich
Town Sq. Iswth —7C
(off Swan St.)
Town Wharf. Iswth —
Toynbee Rd. SW20 —
Trafalgar Av. Wor Pk
Trafalgar Dri. W on T
Trafalgar Rd. Twic —
Tranmere Rd. Twic —
Transport Av. Bren —
Traps La. N Mald —5
Treaty Cen. Houn —1
Trebovir Rd. SW5 —2
Tree Clo. Rich —5E **8**
Treen Av. SW13 —7C
Tregaron Gdns. N Ma
Trehern Rd. SW14 —
Trematon Pl. Tedd —
Trenchard Ct. Mord —
Trentham St. SW18 —
Trent Way. Wor Pk —
Trevanion Rd. W14 —
Treville St. SW15 —4
Trevor Clo. Iswth —2
Trevor Rd. SW19 —4
Trewenna Dri. Chess
Trewince Rd. SW20 —
Triangle, The. King T
Trimmer Wlk. Bren —
Tring Ct. Twic —1B **1**
Trinity Chu. Pas. SW1
Trinity Chu. Rd. SW13
Trinity Clo. Houn —1
Trinity Cotts. Rich —
Trinity Rd. SW19 —3
Trinity Rd. Rich —7G
Trowlock Av. Tedd —
Trowlock Way. Tedd -
Trussley Rd. W6 —1F
Trystings Clo. Clay —
Tucklow Wlk. SW15 -
Tudor Av. Hamp —4F
Tudor Av. Wor Pk —
Tudor Clo. Chess —2
Tudor Ct. Felt —1B **1**
Tudor Ct. Tedd —3A
Tudor Dri. King T —2
Tudor Dri. Mord —3G
Tudor Dri. W on T —
Tudor Gdns. SW13 —
Tudor Gdns. Twic —5
Tudor Rd. Hamp —4F
Tudor Rd. Houn —1J
Tudor Rd. King T —4
Tufton Gdns. W Mol -
Tulip Clo. Hamp —5E
Tunstall Wlk. Bren —
Tunworth Cres. SW15
Turner Av. Twic —7H
Turner Rd. N Mald —
Turneville Rd. W14 —

Grn. Ter. W4 —1B 4
Grn. Ter. M. W4
　　　　—1B 4
am Bri. Twic & Rich
　　　　—2D 8
am Rd. Felt —7E 6
am Rd. Iswth —2B 8
am Rd. Rich —1D 8
am Rd. Tedd
　　　　—1B 14
am Trading Est.
　Iswth —3A 8
v. Twic —7H 7
n Rd. SW19 —7K 17
. Felt —5A 6
Rd. SW6 —5K 5

k. Rd. Tedd —3B 14
Clo. SW15 —1A 16
Cres. SW15 —1A 16
Rd. SW13 —4D 4
SW15 —2G 11
t. SW15 —3D 10
Rich —2F 9
King T —6E 14
l. Iswth —7A 2
k. Rd. W4 —1B 4
Clo. SW14 —2J 9
on Rd. Surb —3E 20
Bren —3D 2
Rd. Eps —7K 25
Rd. W Mol —1E 18
o Rd. Twic —6A 8
Rd. Rich —1E 14
W6 —2D 4
parts)
e Rd. E Mol —7J 13
Rd. King T —3H 15
ond Rd. SW15
　　　　—1C 10
mond Rd. W. Rich &
　SW14 —1H 9
Iswth —7B 2
e. W4 —5H 3
ury Rd. Hamp
　　　　—5D 12
ngton Rd. King T
　　　　—4D 14
. Houn —1F 7
Dri. SW19 —5H 11
Rd. Felt —6B 6
Rd. Hamp —1F 13
Rd. King T —1E 20

s. SW15 —1B 16
.. Clay —5A 24
Clay —5A 24
Eps —7C 22
Sutt —7K 23
Wor Pk —7C 22
N. Surb —6F 21
S. Surb —6F 21
Felt —3A 6
Sun —3A 12
Twic —6A 8
y. Chess —1E 24
dns. SW18 —3J 11
Dri. W on T —3B 18
r Clo. Eps —7K 25
r Rd. Rich —1E 14
Av. N Mald —4A 22
Clo. SW15 —4G 11
Pl. SW6 —4K 5
V. W3 —1G 3
SW6 —4H 5
Hamp —5G 13
i. Twic —2K 7
Av. W6 —1C 4
Clo. Hamp —3D 12
Rd. Th Dit —4C 20
Pl. W6 —1D 4
SW6 —5H 5
dns. W6 —2D 4
d. SW13 —3D 4

Vereker Dri. Sun —7A 12
Vereker Rd. W14 —2H 5
Vermont Rd. Sutt —7K 23
Vernon Av. SW20 —6G 17
Vernon Clo. Eps —3K 25
Vernon Rd. SW14 —7A 4
Vernon St. W14 —1H 5
Verona Dri. Surb —6F 21
Vicarage Dri. SW14 —2A 10
Vicarage Fields. W on T
　　　　—3B 18
Vicarage Rd. SW14 —2A 10
Vicarage Rd. Hamp W —5D 14
Vicarage Rd. King T —6E 14
Vicarage Rd. Sutt —7K 23
Vicarage Rd. Tedd —2B 14
Vicarage Rd. Twic —6K 7
Vicarage Rd. Whit —3H 7
Vickers La. Houn —2D 6
Vickers Way. Houn —2D 6
Victoria Av. Houn —2F 7
Victoria Av. Surb —3E 20
Victoria Av. W Mol —7G 13
Victoria Clo. W Mol —7F 13
Victoria Cotts. Rich —5G 3
Victoria Cres. SW19 —4J 17
Victoria Dri. SW19 —4G 11
Victoria Rd. SW14 —7A 4
Victoria Rd. Felt —5A 6
Victoria Rd. King T —6G 15
Victoria Rd. Surb —3E 20
Victoria Rd. Tedd —3B 14
Victoria Rd. Twic —4C 8
Victoria Vs. Rich —1G 9
Victor Rd. Tedd —1K 13
Victoria Dri. Hamp —3D 12
Victory Bus. Cen. Iswth —1A 8
Viewfield Rd. SW18 —3J 11
Villiers Av. Surb —2G 21
Villiers Av. Twic —5E 6
Villiers Clo. Surb —1G 21
Villiers Path. Surb —2F 21
Villiers Rd. King T —1G 21
Vincam Clo. Twic —4F 7
Vincent Av. Surb —6K 21
Vincent Clo. Esh —7G 19
Vincent Rd. King T —7H 15
Vincent Row. Hamp —3H 13
Vine Clo. Surb —3G 21
Vine Pl. Houn —1G 7
Viner Clo. W on T —3B 18
Vine Rd. SW13 —7C 4
Vine Rd. E Mol —1H 19
Vineyard Hill Rd. SW19
　　　　—1K 17
Vineyard Pas. Rich —2F 9
Vineyard Path. SW14 —7A 4
Vineyard Row. King T —5D 14
Vineyard, The. Rich —2F 9
Viola Av. Felt —3B 6
Virginia Clo. Asht —7E 26
Virginia Clo. N Mald —1K 21
Vivien Clo. Chess —4F 25
Vivienne Clo. Twic —3E 8
Voewood Clo. N Mald —3C 22

Wades La. Tedd —2B 14
Wadham Rd. SW15 —1H 11
Wadhurst Rd. W4 —3K 3
Waight's Ct. King T —5F 15
Wainwright Gro. Iswth —1J 7
Wakefield Rd. Rich —2E 8
Waldeck Rd. W4 —3K 3
Waldeck Rd. SW14 —3H 3
Waldegrave Av. Tedd —2A 14
Waldegrave Gdns. Twic
　　　　—6A 8
Waldegrave Pk. Twic —1A 14
Waldegrave Rd. Twic & Tedd
　　　　—1A 14
Waldemar Av. SW6 —5H 5
Waldemar Rd. SW19 —2K 17

Walham Grn. Ct. SW6 —4K 5
　(off Waterford Rd.)
Walham Gro. SW6 —4K 5
Walham Rise. SW19 —3H 17
Walham Yd. SW6 —4K 5
Walker Clo. Hamp —3E 12
Walkers Pl. SW15 —1H 11
Wallgrave Rd. SW5 —1K 5
Wallorton Gdns. SW14
　　　　—1A 10
Walnut Tree Clo. SW13 —5C 4
Walnut Tree Cotts. SW19
　　　　—2H 17
Walnut Tree Rd. Bren —3F 3
Walpole Av. Rich —6G 3
Walpole Ct. Twic —6K 7
Walpole Cres. Tedd —2A 14
Walpole Gdns. W4 —2K 3
Walpole Gdns. Twic —6K 7
Walpole Pl. Tedd —2A 14
Walpole Rd. Surb —4F 21
Walpole Rd. Tedd —2A 14
Walpole Rd. Twic —6K 7
Walsham Rd. Felt —4A 6
Walters Mead. Asht —6F 27
Walter St. King T —5F 15
Walton Av. N Mald —1C 22
Walton Av. Sutt —7J 23
Walton Pk. W on T —6C 18
Walton Pk. La. W on T
　　　　—6C 18
Walton Rd. W on T & W Mol
　　　　—2B 18
Wanborough Dri. SW15
　　　　—5E 10
Wandle Ct. Eps —1K 25
Wandsworth Bri. Rd. SW6
　　　　—5K 5
Wandsworth High St. SW18
　　　　—2K 11
Wandsworth Plain. SW18
　　　　—2K 11
Wansdown Pl. SW6 —4K 5
Warbank La. King T —4C 16
Warboys App. King T —3J 15
Warboys Rd. King T —3J 15
Warburton Rd. Twic —5G 7
Wardo Av. SW6 —5H 5
Wareham Clo. Houn —1G 7
Warfield Rd. Hamp —5G 13
Warkworth Gdns. Iswth —4B 2
Warner Av. Sutt —6H 23
Warners Clo. Rich —1E 14
Warren Av. Rich —1J 9
Warren Clo. Esh —7G 19
Warren Cutting. King T
　　　　—7F 23
Warren Dri. N. Surb —5J 21
Warren Dri. S. Surb —5K 21
Warren Footpath. —5D 8
Warren Hill. Eps —5K 27
Warren Pk. King T —3K 15
Warren Rise. N Mald —5A 21
Warren Rd. King T —3K 15
Warren Rd. Twic —3H 7
Warren, The. Wor Pk —7A 22
Warrington Rd. Rich —2E 8
Warwick Av. Sutt —6H 23
Warwick Clo. SW15 —4C 10
Warwick Clo. Hamp —4H 13
Warwick Dri. SW15 —7E 4
Warwick Gdns. W14 —1J 5
Warwick Gdns. Asht —6D 26
Warwick Gdns. Th Dit —2A 20
Warwick Gro. Surb —4G 21
Warwick Lodge. Twic —7G 7
Warwick Rd. W14 & SW5
　　　　—1J 5
Warwick Rd. King T —5D 14
Warwick Rd. N Mald —7K 15
Warwick Rd. Th Dit —2A 20
Warwick Rd. Twic —5K 7
Washington Rd. SW13 —4D 4
Washington Rd. King T
　　　　—6H 15
Washington Rd. Wor Pk
　　　　—6E 22

Watchfield Ct. W4 —2K 3
Watcombe Cotts. Rich —3H 3
Waterford Rd. SW6 —4K 5
Watergardens, The. King T
　　　　—3K 15
Waterhouse Clo. W6 —1G 5
Water La. King T —5E 14
Water La. Rich —2E 8
Water La. Twic —5B 8
Waterloo Pl. TW9 —3H 3
Waterloo Pl. Rich —1F 9
Watermans Clo. King T
　　　　—4F 15
Watermans Ct. Bren —3F 3
Waterman St. SW15 —7G 5
Watermill Clo. Rich —7D 8
Water Mill Ho. Felt —6F 7
Watermill Way. Felt —6E 6
Watersedge. Eps —1K 25
Waterside Clo. Surb —6F 21
Waterside Dri. W on T —2A 18
Watersplash Clo. King T
　　　　—7F 15
Waters Rd. King T —6J 15
Waters Sq. King T —7J 15
Watery La. SW20 —6J 17
Watney Rd. SW14 —7K 3
Watson Av. Sutt —6H 23
Watts La. Tedd —2B 14
Watts Rd. Th Dit —4B 20
Wavendon Av. W4 —2A 4
Waverley Av. Surb —3J 21
Waverley Av. Twic —5E 6
Wayneflete Tower Av. Esh
　　　　—7F 19
Wayside. SW14 —2K 9
Wayside Ct. Twic —3D 8
Wealdstone Rd. Sutt —6J 23
Weavers Clo. Iswth —1K 7
Webb Ho. Felt —7D 6
Weimar St. SW15 —7H 5
Weir Rd. W on T —3A 18
Weiss Rd. SW15 —7G 5
Welbeck Clo. N Mald —2C 22
Weldon Dri. W Mol —1E 18
Welford Pl. SW19 —1H 17
Wellesley Av. W6 —1E 4
Wellesley Ct. Sutt —5H 23
Wellesley Cres. Twic —6K 7
Wellesley Pde. Twic —7A 8
Wellesley Rd. W4 —2K 3
Wellesley Rd. Twic —7J 7
Wellington Av. Houn —7J 7
Wellington Av. Wor Pk
　　　　—7F 23
Wellington Ct. Hamp —2J 13
Wellington Cres. N Mald
　　　　—7K 15
Wellington Gdns. Twic
　　　　—1J 13
Wellington Rd. SW19 —6K 11
Wellington Rd. W5 —1D 2
Wellington Rd. Hamp & Twic
　　　　—2J 13
Wellington Rd. N. Houn
　　　　—1E 6
Wellington Rd. S. Houn
　　　　—1E 6
Well La. SW14 —2K 9
Wellmeadow Rd. W7 —1B 2
Wells Ho. Eps —3H 27
Wellside Gdns. SW14 —1K 9
Welstead Way. W4 —1K 3
Welwyn Av. Felt —5J 3
Wendover Dri. N Mald —3C 22
Wensleydale Gdns. Hamp
　　　　—4G 13
Wensleydale Pas. Hamp
　　　　—4F 13
Wensleydale Rd. Hamp
　　　　—4F 13

Wentworth Clo. Surb —6E 20
Wentworth Ct. Twic —7K 7
Werter Rd. SW15 —1H 11
Wessex Av. SW19 —7K 17
Wessex Clo. King T —5J 15
Westbank Rd. Hamp —3H 13
W. Barnes La. N Mald & SW20
　　　　—2E 22
Westbourne Av. Sutt —6H 23
Westbrook Av. Hamp —4E 12
Westbury Av. Clay —3A 24
Westbury Pl. Bren —3E 2
Westbury Rd. Felt —5C 6
Westbury Rd. N Mald —1A 22
West Clo. Hamp —3D 12
Westcoombe Av. SW20
　　　　—5C 16
Westcroft Gdns. Mord —1J 23
Westcroft Sq. W6 —1D 4
W. Cromwell Rd. W14 & SW5
　　　　—2J 5
W. Cross Cen. Bren —3B 2
W. Cross Way. Bren —3C 2
W. Farm Av. Asht —7D 26
W. Farm Clo. Asht —7D 26
Westfield. Asht —7G 27
Westfield Clo. Sutt —7J 23
Westfield Rd. Surb —2E 20
Westfield Rd. Sutt —7J 23
Westfield Rd. W on T —4D 18
Westfields. SW13 —7C 4
Westfields Av. SW13 —7B 4
Westgate Clo. Eps —4K 27
West Gro. W on T —7A 18
Westhay Gdns. SW14 —2J 9
West Hill. SW15 & SW18
　　　　—4G 11
West Hill. Eps —2J 27
W. Hill Av. Eps —2K 27
W. Hill Ct. Eps —2K 27
　(off Court La.)
W. Hill Rd. SW18 —3J 11
Westhorpe Rd. SW15 —7F 5
West La. SW19 —5H 11
W. Kensington Ct. W14
　　　　—2J 5
W. Kensington Mans. W14
　(off Beaumont Cres.) —2J 5
Westlands Ct. Eps
Westleigh Av. SW15 —2E 10
Westmead. SW15 —3E 10
Westminster Clo. Tedd
　　　　—2B 14
Westmoreland Rd. SW13
　　　　—5C 4
Westmorland Clo. Twic —5C 8
Westmorland Ct. Surb —4E 20
West Pk. Av. W on T —1K 3
West Pk. Rd. Rich —5J 3
West Pk. Rd. Eps —1G 27
Westpole Av. Cockf
West Rd. Chess —1D 26
West Rd. SW19 —5J 19
Westmont Rd. Esh —6F 19
W. Side Comn. SW19 —1G 9
W. Temple Sheen. SW14
Westville Rd. Th Dit —5B 20
Westway. SW20 —1E 22

| | | | | |
|---|---|---|---|---|
| Westway Clo. SW20 —7E **16** | Willoughby Rd. Twic —2D **8** | Windmill M. W4 —1B **4** | Woodcote Ho. Eps —4K 27 | Woodward's Footpat |
| Westwood Clo. Esh —7J **19** | Willoughbys, The. SW14 | Windmill Pas. W4 —1B **4** | Woodcote Hurst. Eps —5K 27 | Woolneigh St. SW6 |
| Westwood Gdns. SW13 | —7B **4** | Windmill Rise. King T —4J **15** | Woodcote Pk. Rd. Eps | Wool Rd. SW20 —3 |
| —7C **4** | Willow Av. SW13 —6C **4** | Windmill Rd. SW19 —1E **16** | —5K 27 | Worcester Ct. W on |
| Westwood Rd. SW13 —7C **4** | Willow Bank. SW6 —7H **5** | Windmill Rd. W4 —1B **4** | Woodcote Rd. Eps —3K 27 | Worcester Ct. Wor Pk |
| Wetherby Way. Chess —4F **25** | Willow Bank. Rich —7C **8** | Windmill Rd. W5 & Bren | Woodcote Side. Eps —4J 27 | Worcester Gdns. Wo |
| Wey Ct. Eps —1K **25** | Willow Clo. Bren —3D **2** | —1D **2** | Woodend. Esh —6H **19** | Worcester Pk. Rd. W |
| Weydown Clo. SW19 —5H **11** | Willow Cotts. Rich —3H **3** | Windmill Rd. Hamp —2G **13** | Woodfield. Asht —6E **26** | Worcester Rd. SW19 |
| Weylands Clo. W on T —5E **18** | Willowdene Clo. Twic —4H **7** | Windrush Clo. W4 —5K **3** | Woodfield Clo. Asht —6E **26** | Wordsworth Dri. Sutt |
| Weymouth Av. W5 —1D **2** | Willow End. Surb —5F **21** | Windsor Av. N Mald —2K **21** | Woodfield Gdns. N Mald | Wordsworth Rd. Han |
| Wharfedale St. SW10 —2K **5** | Willow Farm La. SW15 —7E **4** | Windsor Av. Sutt —7H **23** | —2C **22** | Worlidge St. W6 —2 |
| Wharf La. Twic —5B **8** | Willowhayne Dri. W on T | Windsor Av. W Mol —7F **13** | Woodfield La. Asht —6F **27** | Worple Av. SW19 — |
| Whatley Av. SW20 —7G **17** | —4A **18** | Windsor Clo. Bren —3C **2** | Woodfield Rd. Asht —6E **26** | Worple Av. Iswth —2 |
| Wheatfield Way. King T | Willowhayne Gdns. Wor Pk | Windsor Rd. King T —4F **15** | Woodfield Rd. Th Dit —6A **20** | Worple Av. SW20 & |
| —6F **15** | —7F **23** | Windsor Rd. Rich —6G **3** | Woodgate Av. Chess —2E **24** | Worple Rd. Iswth — |
| Wheatley Rd. Iswth —7A **2** | Willow Lodge. SW6 —5F **5** | Windsor Rd. Tedd —2J **13** | Woodhayes Rd. SW19 | Worple Rd. M. SW19 |
| Wheatsheaf La. SW6 —4F **5** | Willow Rd. N Mald —1K **21** | Windsor Rd. Wor Pk —6D **22** | —4F **17** | Worple St. SW14 — |
| Wheatsheaf Ter. SW6 —4J **5** | Willows Path. Eps —3J **27** | Windsor Wlk. W on T —5C **18** | Woodland Dri. Felt —6C **6** | Worple Way. Rich — |
| Wheelers La. Eps —3J **27** | Willow Wlk. Sutt —7J **23** | Windsor Way. W14 —1G **5** | Woodland Gdns. Iswth —7A **2** | Worthington Rd. Sur |
| Whitefield Clo. SW15 —3H **11** | Willow Way. Twic —6G **7** | Windy Ridge Clo. SW19 | Woodlands. SW20 —1F **23** | Worton Ct. Iswth —1 |
| Whitehall Cres. Chess —2E **24** | Wills Cres. Houn —3G **7** | —2G **17** | Woodlands. Asht —7G **27** | Worton Hall Ind. Est. |
| Whitehall Gdns. W4 —3J **3** | Wilmer Clo. King T —2G **15** | Wingfield Rd. King T —3G **15** | Woodlands Av. N Mald | Worton Rd. Iswth — |
| Whitehall Pk. Rd. W4 —3J **3** | Wilmer Cres. King T —2G **15** | Wingrave Rd. W6 —3F **5** | —5K **15** | Wrayfield Rd. Sutt — |
| White Hart La. SW13 —6B **4** | Wilmerhatch La. Eps —7J **27** | Winifred Rd. SW19 —5K **17** | Woodlands Av. Wor Pk | Wraysbury Clo. Houn |
| White Heron M. Tedd —3A **14** | Wilmington Av. W4 —4A **4** | Winifred Rd. Hamp —1F **13** | —6C **22** | Wrights All. SW19 — |
| White Horse Dri. Eps —3K **27** | Wilson Rd. Chess —3G **25** | Winslow Rd. W6 —3F **5** | Woodlands Clo. Clay —4A **24** | Wrights Wlk. SW14 - |
| Whiteley's Cotts. W14 —1J **5** | Wilson's Rd. W6 —2G **5** | Winslow Way. Felt —7D **6** | Woodlands Dri. Sun —6B **13** | Wych Elm Pas. King |
| Whiteley's Way. Felt —7F **7** | Wilson Wlk. W4 —1C **4** | Winslow Way. W on T —7B **18** | Woodlands Ga. SW15 —2J **11** | |
| White Lion Ct. Iswth —7C **2** | (off Prebend Gdns.) | Winston Wlk. W4 —1A **4** | Woodlands Gro. Iswth —6A **2** | Wydell Clo. Mord — |
| Whitestile Rd. Bren —2D **2** | Wilton Av. W4 —2B **4** | Winter Box Wlk. Rich —2G **9** | Woodlands Rd. SW13 —7C **4** | Wyfold Rd. SW6 —4 |
| Whiteswan M. W4 —2B **4** | Wilton Cres. SW19 —4J **17** | Winterfold Clo. SW19 —6H **11** | Woodlands Rd. Eps —4H **27** | Wyke Clo. Iswth —3 |
| Whitlock Dri. SW19 —1J **11** | Wilton Gdns. W on T —5C **18** | Winters Rd. Th Dit —4C **20** | Woodlands Rd. Iswth —6A **2** | Wyke Gdns. W7 —1 |
| Whitmores Clo. Eps —4K **27** | Wilton Gdns. W Mol —7F **13** | Winthorpe Rd. SW15 —1H **11** | Woodlands Rd. Surb —4E **20** | Wyke Rd. SW20 —6 |
| Whitnell Way. SW15 —2F **11** | Wilton Gro. SW19 —4J **17** | Wishford Ct. Asht —7G **27** | Woodlands, The. Esh —5H **19** | Wymond St. SW15 — |
| Whittaker Av. Rich —2E **8** | Wilton Gro. N Mald —3C **22** | Withycombe Rd. SW19 | Woodlands, The. Iswth —6A **2** | Wyncombe Av. W5 – |
| Whittaker Ct. Asht —6E **26** | Wilton Pde. Felt —6A **6** | —4G **11** | Woodlands Way. SW15 | Wyndham Cres. Houn |
| *Whittaker Pl. Rich —2E **8*** | Wilton Row. SW6 —4H **5** | Wivenhoe Ct. Houn —1E **6** | —2J **11** | Wyndham Rd. King T |
| *(off Whittaker Av.)* | Wiltshire Gdns. Twic —5H **7** | Woffington Clo. King T | Woodlands Way. Asht | Wynton Gro. W on T |
| Whittaker Rd. Sutt —7J **23** | Wilverley Cres. N Mald | —5D **14** | —5H **27** | |
| Whittingham Ct. W4 —4B **4** | —3B **22** | Woking Clo. SW15 —1C **10** | Woodland Way. Mord —1J **23** | **X**ylon Ho. Wor Pk — |
| Whittingstall Rd. SW6 —5J **5** | Wimbledon Bri. SW19 —3J **17** | Wolseley Av. SW19 —6K **11** | Woodland Way. Surb —1D **20** | |
| Whitton Dene. Houn & Iswth | Wimbledon Hill Rd. SW19 | Wolseley Gdns. W4 —4J **3** | Wood La. Iswth —3A **2** | **Y**ale Clo. Houn —2E |
| —2H **7** | —3H **17** | Wolseley Rd. W4 —1K **3** | Woodlawn Clo. SW15 —2J **11** | Yardley Ct. Sutt —7F |
| Whitton Mnr. Rd. Iswth | Wimbledon Pk. Rd. SW19 & | Wolsey Av. Th Dit —2A **20** | Woodlawn Cres. Twic —6G **7** | Yeldham Rd. W6 —2 |
| —3H **7** | SW18 —6H **11** | Wolsey Clo. SW20 —4E **16** | Woodlawn Rd. SW6 —4G **5** | Yelverton Lodge. Twi |
| Whitton Rd. Houn —1G **7** | Wimbledon Pk. Side. SW19 | Wolsey Clo. Houn —1H **7** | Woodlawns. Eps —4K **25** | Yenston Clo. Mord — |
| Whitton Rd. Twic —3K **7** | —7G **11** | Wolsey Clo. King T —5J **15** | Woodlodge. Asht —6F **27** | Yeomans M. Iswth — |
| Whitton Waye. Houn —3F **7** | Wimborne Clo. Wor Pk | Wolsey Clo. Wor Pk —7D **22** | Woodside. SW19 —3J **17** | Yew Tree Clo. Wor Pk |
| Wickham Clo. N Mald —3C **22** | —5F **23** | Wolsey Cres. Mord —4H **23** | Woodside Av. Esh —4K **19** | Yew Tree Gdns. Eps |
| Wick Rd. Tedd —4C **14** | Wimpole Clo. King T —6G **15** | Wolsey Dri. King T —2F **15** | Woodside Av. W on T | Yew Tree Wlk. Houn |
| Wicksteed Ho. Bren —2G **3** | Wincanton Rd. SW18 —4J **11** | Wolsey Dri. W on T —5C **18** | —7A **18** | York Av. SW14 —2K |
| Wigley Rd. Felt —6C **6** | Winchelsea Clo. SW15 | Wolsey Rd. E Mol —1J **19** | Woodside Clo. Surb —4K **21** | York Clo. Mord —1K |
| Wilberforce Way. SW19 | —2G **11** | Wolsey Rd. Hamp —3G **13** | Woodside Rd. King T —4F **15** | York Gdns. W on T — |
| —3G **17** | Winchendon Rd. SW6 —5J **5** | Wolsey Way. Chess —2H **25** | Woodside Rd. N Mald —6A **16** | York Pde. Bren —2E |
| Wilcox Rd. Tedd —1J **13** | Winchendon Rd. Tedd —1J **13** | Wolverton Av. King T —5H **15** | Woodspring Rd. SW19 | York Rd. W5 —1D **2** |
| Wildcroft Mnr. SW15 —4F **11** | Winchester Clo. Esh —7F **19** | Wolverton Gdns. W6 —1G **5** | —6H **11** | York Rd. Bren —2E **2** |
| Wildcroft Rd. SW15 —4F **11** | Winchester Clo. King T | Wonford Clo. King T —5B **16** | Woodstock Av. Iswth —2B **8** | York Rd. King T —4C |
| Wilderness, The. Hamp | —4J **15** | Woodbine La. Twic —6J **7** | Woodstock Av. Sutt —4J **23** | York Rd. Rich —2G |
| —1G **13** | Winchester Rd. Felt —7E **6** | Woodbine La. Wor Pk —7F **23** | Woodstock La. N. Surb | York Rd. Tedd —1K |
| Willcocks Clo. Chess —7F **21** | Winchester Rd. Twic —3C **8** | Woodbines Av. King T —7E **14** | —6D **20** | York St. Twic —5B **8** |
| *William Banfield Ho. SW6* | Winchilsea Cres. E Mol | Woodborough Rd. SW15 | Woodstock La. S. Clay & | York Way. Chess — |
| *(off Munster Rd.) —6J **5*** | —6H **13** | —1E **10** | Chess —3C **24** | York Way. Felt —7E |
| William Gdns. SW15 —2E **10** | Windermere Av. SW19 | Woodbourne Dri. Clay | Woodstock Rise. Sutt —4J **23** | (in two parts) |
| *William Morris Ho. W6* | —7K **17** | —3A **24** | Woodstock Rd. W4 —1B **4** | |
| *(off Margravine Rd.) —3G **5*** | Windermere Ct. SW13 —3C **4** | Woodbridge Av. Lea —7B **26** | Wood St. W4 —2B **4** | |
| William Rd. SW19 —4H **17** | Windermere Rd. SW15 | Woodbridge Corner. Lea | Wood St. King T —6E **14** | |
| William's La. SW14 —7K **3** | —1B **16** | —7B **26** | Woodthorpe Rd. SW15 | |
| Willingham Way. King T | Windham Rd. Rich —7G **3** | Woodbridge Gro. Lea —7B **26** | —1E **10** | |
| —7H **15** | Windlesham Gro. SW19 | Woodcote Clo. Eps —3K **27** | Woodview. Chess —7D **24** | |
| Willis Clo. Eps —3J **27** | —5G **11** | Woodcote Clo. King T —2G **15** | Woodview Clo. SW15 —1A **16** | |
| Willmore End. SW19 —5K **17** | Windmill Clo. Surb —5D **20** | Woodcote End. Eps —4K **27** | Woodville Clo. Tedd —1B **14** | |
| Willoughby Rd. King T | Windmill La. Iswth —2A **2** | Woodcote Grn. Rd. Eps | Woodville Rd. Mord —1K **23** | |
| —5G **15** | Windmill La. Surb —3C **20** | —4K **27** | Woodville Rd. Rich —7C **8** | |